CHICKEN SOUP FOR THE FATHER & SON SOUL

Celebrating the Bond That Connects Generations

Jack Canfield
Mark Victor Hansen
Dorothy Firman
Ted Slawski

Health Communications, Inc.
Deerfield Beach, Florida

www.hcibooks.com
www.chickensoup.com

We would like to acknowledge the many publishers and individuals who granted us permission to reprint the cited material. (Note: The stories that were written by Jack Canfield, Mark Victor Hansen, Dorothy Firman, or Ted Slawski are not included in this listing.)

This Magic Moment. Reprinted by permission of Tom Miller.© 2007 Tom Miller.

Saying Good-bye. Reprinted by permission of Tracy K. Crump. © 2007 Tracy K. Crump.

Father's Day. Reprinted by permission of David Avrin. © 2007 David Avrin.

"Little Mike": The Tale of What Really Happened to His Bicycle. Reprinted by permission of Bob Weber. © 2006 Bob Weber.

The Great Rescue. Reprinted by permission of Carol Susan Rothchild. © 2006 Carol Susan Rothchild.

(Continued on page 319)

Scripture quotations marked NKJV are taken from the New King James Version. Copyright © 1982 by Thomas Nelson, Inc. Used by permission. All rights reserved.

In SOQ *Semper Fi,* verses marked TLB are taken from *The Living Bible,* © 1971, Tyndale House Publishers, Wheaton, IL 60189. Used by permission. Used in *Visiting Dad.*

Library of Congress Cataloging-in-Publication Data

Chicken soup for the father & son soul : celebrating the bond that
    connects generations / Jack Canfield ... [et al.].
        p. cm.
    ISBN-13: 978-0-7573-0670-9 (trade paper)
    ISBN-10: 0-7573-0670-5 (trade paper)
    1. Fathers and sons—Anecdotes. 2. Fathers—Anecdotes. 3. Sons—
Anecdotes. 4. Fathers—Conduct of life. I. Canfield, Jack, 1944- II.
Title: Chicken soup for the father and son soul.
HQ755.85.C49716 2008
306.874'2—dc22

                                                          2007052680

Publisher: Health Communications, Inc.
            3201 S.W. 15th Street
            Deerfield Beach, FL 33442-8190

Cover design by Andrea Perrine Brower
Inside formatting by Dawn Von Strolley Grove

11 08

Ted and Didi dedicate this book
to John Winfield Salorio and Steven Wayne Salorio,
the newest father and son in our family.
We have loved our nephew John
since his birth and warmly welcome
his son into the world.

"This is your captain speaking . . .
prepare to soar to great heights, son!"

Contents

Acknowledgments ix

Introduction xiii

1. HOW FATHERS LOVE

This Magic Moment   *Tom Miller* 2

Saying Good-bye   *Tracy Crump* 6

Father's Day   *David Avrin* 9

"Little Mike": The Tale of What Really
    Happened to His Bicycle   *Bob Weber* 13

My Three Sons   *Ted Slawski* 16

The Great Rescue   *Carol S. Rothchild* 18

He Saw Them All   *John C. Spatola* 22

Training Wheels, Training Dad   *Peter Balsino* 24

Ultimate Dad   *Ted Diamond* 28

First, a Father   *David Wilkins* 34

Dad's Gift   *June Williams* 36

2. I LOVE YOU, DAD . . . AND THANKS FOR EVERYTHING

Heritage   *Ed VanDeMark* 41

The Good-Night Kiss   *Helen Kay Polaski* 43

The Big Decision   *John P. Buentello* 47

Saved   *Ted Slawski* 51

Love's Lesson   *Dennis Hixson* 55

What's in a Name? *Joseph Walker*..58

Three Little Words *Don J. Hanson as told to Bonnie Hanson*....................61

The Kind of Man a Boy Needs *Tim Martin* 65

Thanks to the Dragon *Dave Quist* 70

Grass-Cutting Days *Patrick Lyons*..72

The Power of a Son's Kiss *Stephen Wayne* 76

Sharing Love *Julie McMaine Evans*...79

3. WHEN WE WERE YOUNG

Letters to a Teenager *Ken Swarner*...84

Dad's Shadow *Tracy Crump* 87

The End of the Pier *Scott T. Gill*..90

A Father's Christmas Eve Rescue *Nick Walker*........................94

Full House *Win Firman* 97

Things I Learned from My Dad *Bob Smith* 100

This Matchup Will Always Rank as a Classic *Woody Woodburn* 104

Building Your Dreams *Charles E. Harrel*..............................107

One Saturday Morning *Charles E. Harrel*.............................111

Be a Doctor *Paul Winick, M.D.* 115

My Dad Was a Comic Book Hero *Bob Dickson* 120

4. THROUGH WOMEN'S EYES

Lessons from the Dugout *Sarah Smiley*.................................125

One of the Guys . . . at Last *Sally Friedman*.........................128

The Photograph *Dorothy K. Fletcher*....................................131

Strong Arm Needed *Nancy Kay Grace*.................................134

The New Math *Pamela Hackett Hobson* 139

The Fan Club *Sallie Rodman* 141

Three Peas in a Pod *Christine M. Smith*...............................144

Picture Perfect *Sallie Rodman*..147

Not My Father's Son *Ferida Wolff*...151

The Eulogy *Sally Friedman*...153

5. THE CALL OF DUTY

The Last Game *Gary W. Moore* 158

Jumping the Generation Gap *Miriam Hill* 164

Reunion *Win Firman* 168

Semper Fi *Gloria Cassity Stargel* 171

Squeals and Squeezes *Nancy Julien Kopp* 177

One Child, Many Parents *Melissa Moreau Baumann* 179

An Understanding *Robert Anderson* 181

Lessons from My Father *William Garvey* 184

Leadership, Whose Way? *Louis A. Hill, Jr.* 187

The Boys of Iwo Jima *Michael T. Powers* 191

6. TOUGH ROADS, GREAT ACHIEVEMENTS

Daddy Hands *Susan Farr-Fahncke* 196

Lessons Learned at Little League *Glenn Rifkin* 200

He's My Son *Sherry Honeycutt Hatfield* 205

Fathers and Sons and Grandfathers and Angels *Tracey L. Sherman* ...208

Rite of Passage *John Forrest* 212

Visiting Dad *John J. Lesjack* 216

Jason's Story *Carl Ballenas* 221

A Grain of Sand *William Garvey* 225

7. A DAY IN THE LIFE

I Became My Dad Today *Tom Krause* 230

Tuxedo Swimming *Michael T. Powers* 231

Squirrel Wars *Carl Dennison* 234

The Birthday Party *Mark Musolf* 239

Stroller Derby Season *Randy Richardson* 242

Lightning Bugs and Fireworks *Michael T. Powers* 245

Over the Top *Donald Verkow* 247

Kids and Grown-Ups:

   Different as Knight and Day *Randy Richardson* 249

The Son Also Rises *Stephen Lautens* 252

Father to Son *Joseph Walker* 256

The Walk of Life *Matthew Favreault* 259

Pinewood Derby *Ken Swarner*...264
The Giants *Michael Fulton*..267

8. THE WISDOM OF ALL AGES

Hands of Time *Gary B. Xavier*..271
The Invitation *John J. Lesjack*...274
Just a Little Bit Longer *Frederick Bakowski*.........................278
Rediscovered Hero *Joseph Walker*......................................282
The Grandpa Who Became a Daddy *Patricia Lorenz*...........285
Morning Peace *Andy Radujko*...289
The Winner *Calvin Riendeau*..291
Going Fishing with Grandpa *Woody Woodburn*...................293
I'll Tell Him Tomorrow *Lanny Zechar*.................................296
It's Good to Be Here *Joseph Walker*...................................299

More Chicken Soup?...303
Supporting Others..304
Who Is Jack Canfield?..305
Who Is Mark Victor Hansen?..306
Who Is Dorothy Firman?..307
Who Is Ted Slawski?..308
Contributors..309
Permissions *(continued)*...319

Acknowledgments

We wish to express our heartfelt gratitude to the following people who helped make this book possible.

Our families, who have been chicken soup for our souls!

Jack's family, Inga, Travis, Riley, Christopher, Oran, and Kyle, for all their love and support.

Mark's daughter, Elisabeth Del Gesso, and her son, Seth (Mark's grandson!), and his daughter, Melanie Hansen, for once again sharing and lovingly supporting us in creating yet another book.

Dorothy Firman and Ted Slawski thank their fathers, Winfield Firman and the late Ted Slawski, who have guided and supported us through our lives; our sons, Jody and Tom and Chris, each of whom has taught us about fathers and sons and given us great joy; the women in our lives, our mothers, Julie Firman and the late Katherine Slawski; our daughter, Sarah; and the next generation, Sarah Slade, Mia Rose and Isabella Ivy Goodbar, and those grandchildren to come, giving us faith in the future and reminding us of the beauty and love that is always here.

Our publisher and friend, Peter Vegso, for his continuous support and allegiance to all of us and to the Chicken Soup brand.

Patty Aubery and Russ Kamalski, for being there on

every step of the journey with love, laughter, and endless creativity.

Barbara LoMonaco, for nourishing us with truly wonderful stories and cartoons.

D'ette Corona, our coauthor liaison, who seamlessly manages twenty to thirty projects at a time.

Patty Hansen, for her thorough and competent handling of the legal and licensing aspects of the Chicken Soup for the Soul books. You are magnificent at the challenge!

Veronica Romero, Lisa Williams, Teresa Collett, Robin Yerian, Jesse Ianniello, Lauren Edelstein, Lauren Bray, Patti Clement, Michelle Statti, Debbie Lefever, Connie Simoni, Karen Schoenfeld, Catalie Chen, Patti Coffey, Lauren Mastrodonte, Gina Rose Kimbull, and Lindsay Schoenfeld, who support Jack's and Mark's businesses with skill and love.

Laurie Hartman, Dee Dee Romanello, and Patti Clement, who support our Costa Mesa operation with skill and love.

Michele Matriscini, Carol Rosenberg, Andrea Gold, Allison Janse, Katheline St. Fort, our editors at Health Communications, Inc., for their devotion to excellence.

Lori Golden, Kelly Maragni, Sean Geary, Patricia McConnell, Kim Weiss, Paola Fernandez-Rana, Christine Zambrano, and Jaron Hunter, for doing such an incredible job supporting our books.

Tom Sand, Claude Choquette, and Luc Jutras, who manage year after year to get our books translated into thirty-six languages around the world.

Larissa Hise Henoch, Lawna Patterson Oldfield, Andrea Perrine Brower, Anthony Clausi, Peter Quintal, Justin Rotkowitz, and Dawn Von Strolley Grove for their talent, creativity, and unrelenting patience while producing book covers and inside designs that capture the essence of Chicken Soup.

Our glorious panel of readers who helped us make the final selections and made invaluable suggestions on how to improve the book: Ayla Wickham-Diemand, Alex and Nick Leras, Rose and Arthur Quinton, Pat Pruyne, Rebecca Aronson, Ann and Bob Grose, Kathleen Howell, Gene Tansey, Shirley Packard, Win Firman, Peter and Pat Rowland, Myra Berzoff, Gloria and Fred Ayvazian, Frances Salorio, Edie Cutler, Jennifer Dale, Michele Edelstein, Tracy Farnham, Swannee Bruner, Chris Dahl, Heather Perkins, Daphne Slocombe, Melanie Johnson, Heather Lindsay, Heidi Keller, and Sallie Rodman.

To everyone who submitted a story, we deeply appreciate your letting us into your lives and sharing your experiences with us. For those whose stories were not chosen for publication, we hope the stories you are about to enjoy convey what was in your heart and in some way also tell your stories.

Because of the size of this project, we may have left out the names of some people who contributed along the way. If so, we are sorry, but please know that we really do appreciate you very much.

We are truly grateful and love you all!

Introduction

The story of fathers and sons is every man's story . . . and a story that every woman participates in. It is the story of love, courage, mentoring, sacrifice, challenge, loss, pain, and redemption. It is every story: the first-time father holding his newborn son; the baseball games, bike rides, hikes; the tension, the fights, and disappointments. It is a father and son, now adults, carving out a new relationship. It is family growing as new generations come. It is the son at his father's grave—and so tragically, sometimes the father at his son's grave. Throughout it all, even in the face of difficulties and loss, the son carries his father within, as an image of who men are, as someone to be just like, or as someone to be different from. The father's impact on his son carries on for generations as each new father tries to take the best his father gave him and pass it on to his son. At the same time, that new father struggles to find his own way, to be his own man. And so boys become men, men become fathers, fathers help mold their sons, and the cycle continues.

No perfect father or perfect son exists, but everyone carries the profound importance of the father-son relationship within. For those of us who are men, we have all lived deeply and closely as fathers and sons, learning wise lessons and learning hard lessons. We have known ourselves as sons, building our lives in ways great and small around our fathers (or the many father substitutes that play this all-important role). We remember ourselves as boys and know how we loved our fathers. We know when we made them proud, and we know when we didn't. We know what it is like to carry our fathers within and to become the best men we can be. For men who have had sons, we continue that cycle, giving it our best shot, knowing only too well that we sometimes fall short of our own ideal. We never stop loving our sons, and we always see, just a little bit, our own selves in their lives.

For those of us who are women, we have seen in our brothers and fathers and grandfathers, in our sons and husbands, in our friends and strangers, what a father and son are. We know them at their best, and, as we know ourselves likewise, we know them in their imperfection. And throughout our lives with fathers and sons, we see how special that relationship is. We also find our place in it. We are the wives and mothers, sisters and daughters, grandmothers and great-grandmothers who walk side by side with the fathers and sons we love.

Gathering the stories of so many fathers and sons has been a gift as we watch our own children leave the nest and begin a new generation of families that will carry us within them as the future continues to unfold. Our thanks to fathers and sons throughout the world for doing their best to make the world a better place. It is our deepest wish that all people might live in peace.

Dorothy Firman and Ted Slawski

1

HOW FATHERS LOVE

My father used to play with my brother and me in the yard. My mother would come out and say, "You're tearing up the grass!" "We're not raising grass," my dad would reply. "We're raising boys."

Harmon Killebrew

This Magic Moment

A baby is God's opinion that the world should go on.

Carl Sandburg

I never imagined myself as a parent until the moment, twenty-four years ago, that my son was born. But then, I never believed in magic either. I knew that my wife wanted children, but I couldn't quite understand why. She wanted four or five, I seem to remember. I do know that it was a big number—big enough that I didn't take her seriously.

Eventually, my wife prevailed and I agreed to try one, like we were considering potato chips. Once the decision was made, I pushed it aside. After all, nothing is certain. One of us could be sterile. If not, it still might take years to conceive. Why borrow trouble? Why, indeed?

Talk about miscalculation. It took us no time at all—a couple of months at most from decision to conception. When my wife became ill in the middle of *Das Boot* and rushed out of the theater, I experienced a sinking feeling. And it had nothing to do with the fate of the German submarine. I guess I slipped into denial after that. Throughout her pregnancy, even when fatherhood was imminent, the idea remained far-fetched—at best, abstract. But isn't magic always that way?

My denial notwithstanding, things were different around our place. My wife cast an ever larger and more awkward shadow when she stood outside with the dogs. Early every Saturday morning for weeks, we stumbled off to Lamaze class, where we dutifully sat on the floor, surrounded by pillows, and breathed together. I silently hoped that I didn't look as silly as I felt. Every time I checked, there was something new (and miniature) in the spare bedroom. The evidence was piling up, but I was trying hard not to notice.

On February 21, 1983, my wife made her final scheduled visit to the doctor. He assured her that the baby would arrive in two weeks—right on schedule. Yeah, right. At 5:00 the next morning, my wife awoke with a start. On those rare occasions when I had faced reality, however fleetingly, it always happened this way—late in the night when the fog of sleep was thickest. Even as it dawned on me what was happening, I tried to resist. "Okay," I said, "I'll start some coffee and call the doctor." No, I didn't have it backward. I couldn't have a baby without caffeine. The doctor told me what I wanted to hear. No rush. Have your coffee, get dressed, and get to the hospital.

We left for the hospital by 6:00. It was still dark, and a cold rain was falling. It made for a gloomy drive, but things could have been much worse. This was February in Iowa. We were lucky it wasn't snowing. Then I remembered: it was February 22—Washington's birthday. I wondered out loud that if we had a boy, perhaps we should name him George. I was only teasing, but my wife wasn't the least bit amused. We had long ago agreed upon David Thomas and Sarah Elizabeth as names and that was that.

I was about to protest when I remembered the two words my best man had told me always worked with wives, and I repeated them. "Yes, dear."

At the hospital, someone whisked my wife off to a room while I stayed behind to check her in. It was early, and the reception area and adjacent waiting room were nearly deserted. As I filled out form after form, each repeating the same questions, I made a mental list of things I needed to do. I couldn't believe I was thinking so clearly—and after a single cup of coffee. I still didn't get it!

By the time I had finished with the forms, my wife was settled into a room upstairs. I hurried up to find that there was no need to hurry. The contractions had just begun and were far apart. I wouldn't be a father for a while. Things moved slowly through the morning, and I wondered if this wasn't a false alarm. But misdirection is the magician's ally. Then in the early afternoon, my wife's blood pressure spiked. It was obvious in the way the nurses unceremoniously shooed me away that they were alarmed. Shortly, the doctor hurried into the room. As I stood helplessly off to the side, a small drama unfolded in the cramped room.

The doctor gave my wife a shot to speed things along, and the nurses wheeled her away, with me trailing anxiously behind. *A fifth wheel*, I thought. Inside the delivery room, I stood beside my wife, holding her hand and encouraging her. The birth was over in no time, its quickness startling me after long hours of prelude. I looked up at a clock mounted on the far wall. It was 3:30—and in that precise moment, I became a believer. In magic. A nurse had wrapped our new son in a blanket and passed him to me. *Our son! Our. Son.* I wanted to prolong the moment, fearing that the magic, like time, was ephemeral. I shouldn't have worried. I kissed him gently on the forehead. Over the years, I must have repeated that ritual fifty thousand times: when he woke up in the morning, at odd times during the day, and before I tucked him in at night.

In that instant, I was transformed so suddenly and so completely that nothing could explain it except magic. This little person I held had been in the world only a precious few minutes, but I already loved him in a way I didn't know was possible—that I could scarcely comprehend. What was that if not magic? There could be no other explanation.

Twenty-four years later, nothing has happened to change my mind. If anything, I am even more convinced. Our son has grown up and moved away, but the magic remains my constant companion. It's homesteaded in my heart, you see.

Tom Miller

Saying Good-bye

Let us be grateful to people who make us happy.
They are the charming gardeners who make our
souls blossom.

Marcel Proust

Stan pulled the moving-van door closed and wiped his sweaty face. "Whew! We're finally done."

I smiled and took my husband's hand as we trudged toward the back door. "Who would have thought a nine-by-eleven–foot bedroom could hold enough to fill a sixteen-foot truck?"

Inside, we walked to our older son's nearly empty room and found him stuffing the last of his clothes into a suitcase.

"Well, tomorrow's the big day. Soon you'll be in your new apartment." Stan enveloped Brian in a bear hug.

Brian grinned and hugged his dad back.

Some fathers have difficulty expressing affection for their sons. My husband is not one of them. When our two boys were young, Stan did all the guy things with them—wrestled and roughhoused, played sports, and built things—but he never hesitated to heap plenty of hugs and kisses on them, too. So it was no surprise to me that my husband's demonstrations of love continued as they got older. The boys willingly returned his embraces. They had never known any other way.

The next day, we loaded the rest of Brian's things into his Ford Escort and headed our convoy toward Atlanta, where graduate school awaited. Brian's four years in college had flown by. Now ready to test his wings, he eagerly anticipated living on his own, seven hours away from home.

A flurry of unpacking, cleaning, and shopping followed our arrival. Stan and our younger son, Jeremy, installed track lighting in the poorly lit living room. Brian arranged books on his new shelves, and I stocked kitchen cabinets. Before long, the apartment looked almost lived-in.

The next morning, I was all set to start the trip home, but Stan seemed to drag out our departure. I tried to be patient and busy myself with more cleaning and straightening, but my tolerance evaporated when I saw Stan and Brian head out the door at 11:00 AM. "Where are you two going?"

"Home Depot to get another lamp for the bedroom. We'll be back soon."

Two hours later, they returned with armloads of more furnishings to assemble. It was 3:00 PM before we exchanged our final hugs and kisses and got into the car. Stan started the engine, and we pulled out of the parking space. When I turned to wave one more time, I saw a look on Brian's face that explained Stan's reluctance to leave. The bravado was gone. The excitement of living on his own had collided with reality, and he looked like a lost little boy.

It was a long trip home.

If parting was tough on Brian, it was even tougher on Stan. For two weeks he hardly slept and admitted that he often woke up in a cold sweat, dreaming something had happened to his son. Stan made excuses to call Brian several times a day because he'd suddenly remembered something he "forgot to tell him"—things like when to change his oil filter or how to hang a picture or some equally weighty matter. He appeared to find comfort in hearing Brian's voice, but the words they always used to say good-bye cheered him the most.

"I love you, Brian."

"I love you, too, Dad."

Slowly the pain of separation lessened, and Brian weaned his dad to one phone call a day. After Brian made a quick trip home for Labor Day weekend, Stan slacked off to three or four calls a week. Each conversation, however, ended the same way.

"I love you, Brian."

"I love you, too, Dad."

Two months after our son's move, Stan was almost back to normal. He called Brian one Friday evening for a now-weekly chat. Hearing voices in the background, Stan asked where he was.

"I'm at a restaurant with friends from church. Can I call you back tomorrow?"

"Sure." Determined not to humiliate Brian by wringing an "I love you" from him, Stan abstained from his usual closing and ended the conversation with "Talk to you later. 'Bye."

The next day, Brian called his dad. With a note of indignation in his voice, he asked, "Why didn't you say 'I love you' last night?"

Stan stammered. "I didn't want to embarrass you in front of your friends."

"If my friends don't like me saying 'I love you' to my dad, that's *their* problem. But I expect *you* to say 'I love you.' Got it?"

"Got it!"

"I love you, Dad."

"I love you, too, Brian."

Tracy Crump

Father's Day

For *everything that lives is holy, life delights in life.*

William Blake

"Hey, Bubba," I shout to my three-year-old son from the couch in my family room. "C'mere a minute."

At once, I hear the familiar and rapid *thump, thump, thump* as he comes bounding into the room, a bent paper towel roll in one hand and a fistful of crayons in the other.

"Yeah, Dad?" he inquires as I pull him onto my lap.

"Mom is taking your sisters to go buy jeans, so you and I get 'Special Time' together at home!"

"Just us?" he asks with wide-eyed surprise and a big smile.

"Just us," I confirm. "What do you want to do?" I ask, expecting a request for some variation of crash-'em-up wrestling or playing with his little plastic farm animals.

Spencer stands up and thinks for a moment, tapping his finger on his chin—mimicking my gesture. A huge smile erupts on his face as he rushes out of the room, only to appear moments later with a large, half-unraveled roll of bubble-wrap spilling out of his arms and dragging on the floor.

"You want to pop bubbles?" I ask, confused.

"And watch a movie!" he adds enthusiastically.

Spencer turns and rummages through the DVDs like a pirate on a treasure hunt. He emerges moments later triumphantly waving a copy of the animated hit *The Incredibles* high in the air.

"Okay," I say, smiling. He loves the movie and fancies himself "Dash," the young son of Mr. Incredible, with incredible powers of his own. When he and I play superheroes, he is Dash—naturally, I'm Mr. Incredible.

Like some kind of techno-wizard, as virtually all three-year-olds are these days, he ejects the DVD drawer from the player, inserts the movie, expertly navigates through the on-screen menu, and hits play.

He then rushes back to the couch and jumps into my lap. As the movie begins, we grab the bubble wrap and go to town on those helpless little plastic-covered pockets of air. They don't stand a chance.

For over an hour and a half, Spencer and I sit on the couch, snap bubbles, and immerse ourselves in the movie.

If anyone else were in the room, the constant popping sound would drive them out of their mind. But tonight, it is just me and my little Bubba, and we are having a blast!

When my arm begins to fall asleep, I stretch for the ceiling; Spencer nuzzles in a little closer. *Snap. Snap.* I squeeze his little legs and he giggles. *Snap. Snap.*

For a full ten seconds, our popping is precisely in unison and we laugh. He tries to snap the bubbles as fast as he can—his pudgy little arms tensing and releasing. I wrap him a little tighter in my arms.

I'm lost in the moment and, thinking back, I can feel my own father's arms envelop me when I sat in his lap. I wonder if Spencer will remember this night and feel the same comfort, security, and love that I found in my daddy's arms—so long ago.

Spencer isn't just sitting on my lap. No, my son sits *in* my lap. My tactile little man nuzzles into every nook, cranny, fold, and crevice his little body can wriggle into.

For an hour and a half, the two of us hardly say a word. We just watch the adventure unfold on the screen as we unconsciously unfold new sections of bubble wrap. Our fingers mindlessly search for bubbles until we can't find any more. Then we simply toss the mangled plastic wrap to the side and snuggle even closer just as Mr. Incredible is captured by the evil Syndrome. Spencer's fingers slide between mine and he holds on tight.

That night I tune-out every work-related stress and pending "to do" list and immerse myself in my squishy little boy and drink up his company.

And just as he does every time, Mr. Incredible and his family save the day. As the credits roll, I peek around from the side and discover Spencer's eyes are closed, his face so peaceful. I click the TV remote, and as the screen goes black, I just sit with him, quietly. It doesn't matter what the calendar says. For me, today is Father's Day.

David Avrin

"Little Mike": The Tale of What Really Happened to His Bicycle

The question for each man to settle is not what he would do if he had the means, time, influence and educational advantages, but what he will do with the things he has.

Hamilton Wright Mabie

It was over sixty years ago, and I remember the day Dad brought home that muddy, broken piece of rusted junk he called a bicycle. Dad was always bringing home old stuff and fixing it up. He was a real craftsman. He said it was his way to keep his mind off the "bad stuff." He was a Ramsey County deputy sheriff in Minnesota.

I didn't have a bike, but it was very clear in my mind that this beat-up derelict wasn't the kind of bike I planned to own. Mine would have glistening chrome wheels, a rearview mirror, plus an electric headlight, and horn. Maybe even a siren!

Mom started complaining about that "piece of junk" leaning against the side of the house. Dad explained, with the saddest face I have ever seen, that he had recently encountered a little boy who had lost his parents in a tragic accident. Dad called him "Little Mike" and said he was about my age.

He further explained that Little Mike had been placed in the county orphanage. Whenever we drove by that orphanage and Dad would point out Little Mike's room, I would insist that we stop. I wanted to see him, be his friend. Dad would decline, telling me we had more urgent chores to do that day. I always left on the verge of tears.

Dad seemed unusually concerned about Little Mike and mentioned him often. The boy had lost everything! He said he had a plan that might help Little Mike feel a little less lonely and asked if I would like to help. His plan was simple. He was going to fix up that junky old bike and present it to Little Mike as a surprise. I thought it was a super idea!

We began the makeover. We sanded off the faded paint and rust down to mirror-bright bare metal. My father was a magician with a paintbrush and the gleaming new paint job looked great. Together we hunted for all kinds of replacement parts. We polished the chrome. Dad carefully replaced bent and broken spokes. He taught me how to install a new chain. We did a terrific job! He asked me what else could be added. I quickly volunteered that a rearview mirror, electric headlight, and horn would be super. We quickly added them. What a beauty!

I was excited! The long anticipated moment had arrived. We were finally ready to deliver the bike to its unsuspecting new owner. *That never happened.*

You see, there never was a tragic accident, there never was a county orphanage, and most of all, there never was a Little Mike. It just happened that the day this glorious gift was to be delivered was also my birthday.

The project in which I had so willingly participated over

these many weeks was an elaborate charade concocted by Mom and Dad to surprise me with a bike for my birthday. Their major concern was how the bike could be a birthday surprise and yet be hidden from me for what they knew would be at least three months of evenings during the restoration process. "Little Mike" was their answer. The sell job they did on me would make any award-winning actor pale by comparison.

The time Dad and I spent together is unforgettable. It's what they now call "quality" time. I loved that bicycle but often wish there really had been a "Little Mike."

Bob Weber

My Three Sons

I was eight when *My Three Sons* first appeared on TV. I watched it a few times, but I was more of a *Combat!* kind of kid. By the time I was eighteen, I'd seen it enough times to say out loud, many times, "Never. Not me, man."

I was convinced I'd have no kids. *Good plan*, I thought. *The world is overpopulated, kids take up your whole life, I'd be a lousy father* . . . (At eighteen I didn't have the all-time best relationship with my father, which certainly colored my view of the world of parenting.)

Ever hear the joke, "How do you make God laugh?" (Answer: Make a plan.) Before I was nineteen, I was in love with the woman who is still my wife more than thirty years later. I knew then it was true love and time has proven me right. *But* . . . she came fully equipped with a son. A package deal; all or nothing. Do I give up the love of my life? "Daddy" didn't sound too bad.

I actually liked the little rug rat, and I slipped by the first milestone in my now-compromised plan. In fact, at our wedding, when little Jody got restless, my wife-to-be-in-five-minutes and I held him between us during the ceremony.

There are women who will have a child and feel done and then there are women who are *mothers eternally*. My darling was of the later genus. She was dead set on having another child. In fact she was set on having one with me. And over a few years, she, of course, won. (Anybody surprised?) When my first child, a daughter, was born, I cried for the first time since I was a young boy. "I can do this. She's a girl. They gotta be easy, right?"

We were actually content to have our two children, one of each gender. *Perfect,* I thought.

I don't understand women, but about five years after our daughter was born, when we should have been putting money into a retirement account, my wife sidled up to me and said, "Don't you want a little boy? A little Teddy Bear?" which was her pet nickname for me.

"Ah . . . no, thank you, dear," I exclaimed loudly and clearly while running out of the house on some nonexistent errand.

Saying something like that to a dyed-in-the-wool, certified mother is about as effective as explaining to the dog what part of the yard to use for the bathroom. True to (her) plan, our son was born two years later. I didn't cry this time, but Tom was born in distress and ended up in Boston Children's Hospital. But after a good scare, which turned out to be a minor problem, he was a healthy baby.

Yep, he was fine, and surprisingly, so was I. I even ended up being the househusband for a few years when I was laid off. I loved that kid. I loved all three of them.

Many years later, I happened to think of that old TV show, for no particular reason, and thought to myself, *At least I don't have three sons!*

Hah! Me and my big mouth. A month later, my then twenty-five-year-old daughter introduced me to my next son—her soon-to-be husband, Chris.

I walked her down the aisle, but I didn't give her away. I let her give me my third son. And, yeah, I love him, too.

Ted Slawski

The Great Rescue

No man stands so straight as when he stoops to help a boy.

Knights of Pythagoras

It is nothing short of amazing to watch a child and see glimmers of a parent. Sometimes it's just an expression or a gesture that suddenly reveals itself as familiar. Yet it is with frustration and eye rolling that I tell myself that my nine-year-old son, Alex, is his father's boy. He'll spend two hours on his homework and forget to hand it in. He'll run upstairs to take a shower and wind up sitting in his room with some electronic toy in hand. He really means to get those clothes in the hamper . . .

One morning Alex was spending a little quality time with his hamster, Bamboo, before the start of the school day. I yelled up the stairs in the midst of the usual morning turmoil, "Let's go, Alex! Shoes on. Get your lunch. We have to go!" Nothing seemed out of the ordinary when a few minutes later Alex came flying down the steps initiating the search for his sneakers.

Several hours later, when I walked into his bedroom, the

glimmer appeared. My little absentminded professor had forgotten to put the cover back on his hamster's cage. *Bamboo is probably just asleep under the shavings,* I told myself hesitantly. I nudged a few shavings. No hamster. Uh-oh. I dug through those shavings, parting clusters of bedding like a bulldozer. And then reality hit. Hamster on the loose!

I called my husband at work, since I thought he could relate firsthand to the absentmindedness. He suggested that I put a little food in each room to figure out where our fur ball might be. "Don't worry," he assured me. "Bamboo will appear."

"I hope so," I responded. "And I really hope it's before the school bus does."

When Alex came home from school, I tried to be nonchalant. "Honey, you left the cover off Bamboo's cage." His eyes widened. "But I called Dad, and he said not to worry. Bamboo is friendly and smart. We'll find him."

"Oh, no!" he yelled, and bolted up the steps in search of his pet.

The search went on and on, and then at bedtime Alex just broke down. "It's my fault," he sobbed. "Bamboo could dehydrate; he could be trapped; he could be dead." I couldn't fix this one, no matter how much I assured him that we all make mistakes and Bamboo might be okay. He was inconsolable, and I realized that this weight he carried, this responsibility for another life, had made his heart heavy. I lay down next to him, engulfed in my own helplessness, as he cried and cried, then finally fell asleep.

It was around 2:00 AM when I awoke to the sound of Alex and his dad. I sat up, unable to comprehend why anyone would be up at this hour. I walked into Alex's room, and my husband excitedly explained, "I was downstairs when I heard him in the ceiling. He must have fallen through a tiny hole in Alex's floor that surrounds a pipe. Now he's trapped."

Alex, as awake as ever, said, "Mom, he's alive!"

I sat down on the edge of his bed and watched while my husband moved Alex's dresser and squished his six-foot two-inch frame into the little work area he had made for himself. And then, with saw in hand, he began to enlarge the opening in the floor. *My husband is cutting up the floor now,* I thought to myself. *What next? 9-1-1 rescue team?*

"I hope Bamboo has the sense to stay away from this falling sawdust," he muttered.

Only I thought it odd that we were all up in the middle of the night cutting up the floor. This seemingly endless carpentry feat took only about twenty minutes, at which time the Search and Rescue Team shined a flashlight down the newly modeled hole.

"Alex! Come here!" my husband bellowed.

"What is it, Dad?"

"It's Bamboo! I see him!"

Alex maneuvered himself into that diminutive crawl space, like some *Alice in Wonderland* character, clutching his flashlight. He aimed his light down into the hole. He smiled. "I see him, Dad! I see him! But how do we get him out?"

The effort continued. Alex was just able to fit his arm down through the hole, but Bamboo would not cooperate. "It's really cold down there," Alex reported. "This isn't good." Next they detached a toy ladder from its shiny red truck, lowered it carefully within the hole, and waited. Bamboo, always up for the challenge of a good climb, would not perform.

Oh God, I thought to myself. *What if they just can't do this? What if Bamboo really does freeze to death or dehydrate down there?* I watched them in silence as they plotted their next move.

"Alex, go get a carrot and a string," his dad advised. "It's time to get this hamster." Within seconds, Alex arrived with the goods and watched as his dad attached the carrot to the line and lowered it into darkness. Alex held the flashlight. They waited and waited. "No sign of him," my husband reported.

"Alex, come back to bed," I pleaded. "Tomorrow is a school day. This is crazy."

"I can't go to school tomorrow," he told me, eyes bright with fear. "Not if Bamboo isn't safe!"

He should not be getting his hopes up like this, I thought. *What are the odds of retrieving a tiny, trapped fur ball with a mind of his own?*

"Ssh!" my husband whispered. Carefully he lifted the string. It seemed to come up in slow motion, like a fish line taut with anticipation. And there he was, Bamboo, dangling by his mouth, pouching that carrot for dear life. "Hold your hamster," he said to Alex. "He really missed you."

Alex sat on the edge of his bed. His smile was back. He hugged Bamboo. He kissed Bamboo. Peace was restored in my house. It was on the tip of my tongue to say, *Do you realize how lucky you are? Do you realize that most dads wouldn't cut through the floor in the middle of the night to find a lost hamster? Do you realize your father is one in a million?* But I stopped myself in time.

"Thank you, Daddy," he whispered.

Carol S. Rothchild

He Saw Them All

The truest greatness lies in being kind, the truest wisdom in a happy mind.

Ella Wheeler Wilcox

My love for baseball comes from my father. He took me to Yankee and Met games. He taught me how to hit from both sides of the plate. I was a good hitter.

Dad signed me up for Gil Hodges Little League in 1970. In my first year, I held my own. By my second year, I was trying so hard to make my father proud I would strike out every time he came to a game. My dad would always tell me to keep my head up and not give up. He also realized I was trying too hard to impress him. When he told me he had to work and couldn't come to any more games that year, I was really upset. But I managed to hit four home runs in the next five games. Dad never got to see them.

In the final game of the year I came up. With two outs in the last inning and the bases loaded, we were down 6-3. I looked in the stands and saw my dad peeking out from behind the concession stand. I was determined to hit one home run Dad would see. I took three balls and I knew the pitcher could not walk me. He threw one and I hit it over the 180-foot right field fence. I looked for dad but he was gone. After the game, he pulled up with the car, smiled, and asked me how I did.

"Dad," I said, "I saw you in the stands behind the concessions."

"Wow, you did?" he said. "What a shot you hit! I think that was the longest home run you've hit yet."

And then I got it. He'd been there every time, watching—and hiding—giving me the best chance I could ever have to do my best. And I did.

John C. Spatola

Training Wheels, Training Dad

To exist is to change, to change is to mature, to mature is to go on creating oneself endlessly.

Henri Bergson

"I'll call you names, too, if you keep calling me names," my six-year-old son blurted through his tears.

Not my proudest moment as a father. I had been badgering him all morning, trying to push him past his fear of riding his bike without training wheels. How could he be afraid? Of all my kids, he had always been the daredevil. More important, who was this monster calling his son names like "quitter" and "chicken"? This moment had been building since July, when Taylor turned six. Most kids—the neighborhood kids anyway—had been riding two-wheelers since they were four years old.

I think the fact that I had always taken pride in Taylor's bold personality and natural athletic ability only compounded my frustration. From the moment he was born, Taylor was a father's dream. He was never without some kind of a ball, and proved every day that he was all "snips and snails and puppy dog tails."

The plain truth was that Taylor had spoiled me. I'd gotten used to eating up other dads' envy as they watched Taylor try some athletic skill for the first time. Taylor needed to be shown something only once and he could do it. I was certain he could already ride. He was just afraid.

But that's the part that just didn't compute. I couldn't fathom how Taylor could be afraid, not this boy who attempted stunts that would make Evel Knievel cringe.

By the end of September I'd had it! We were well into the middle of the flag football season, and I had spent the past four Saturdays watching this boy dive for flags, block the heck out of older boys twice his size, and run for touchdowns. On each corresponding Sunday, however, this same boy whined, faked injuries, and refused to even try to ride his bike.

Infected by pride, I decided that the end justifies the means. The following weekend, I swore that Taylor would leave the park on his own and on two wheels. We went through our usual routine of Taylor's panicking each time I let go of his seat and either falling or diving off his bike. I'm not proud of it, but I snapped.

Despite promises I had made myself when Taylor was born, I transformed into Robert Duvall in *The Great Santini*. For those who aren't part of this 1979 movie's cult following, it's about a legendary tough-as-nails fighter pilot and his relationship with his family. The scene that always sticks with me as a father is the fight Santini starts with his teenage son after he loses to him at basketball for the first time. As the son walks away to defuse the situation, Santini keeps bouncing the ball off the back of his son's head while repeating something like "You're my favorite little girl."

Taylor managed to maintain his composure while I threatened to throw his bike into a trash can. "Well, if you're not going to ride it, I might as well throw it away," I scolded.

That classy maneuver bought me another attempt. After his fear made him lose his balance, he sprang up clutching his banged knee and pleaded, "There, I tried. Can we go home now?" I guess that's when the name-calling started.

A rabies vaccine couldn't have worked any better than Taylor's diplomatic approach to my irrational behavior. Rather than retaliate, he wanted me to realize that I wouldn't like it if he called me names. I was floored. For once, I was the one who needed a "time-out."

I rushed over and hugged Taylor tight. "I shouldn't have called you names. That was wrong, and I won't do it again," I assured him. "You can keep riding with your training wheels on as long as you want."

When we returned home, all I wanted was to get back into Taylor's good graces. I knew just how to do it. Tools. Taylor loves tools! I took him into the garage to help me put his training wheels back on. We put on the matching tool belts that my wife had given us for Christmas the year before. Knowing he'd be disappointed with just a wrench, I also let him take a screwdriver, hammer, and a pair of pliers. As I handed him each tool, he looked up at me with undying gratitude. Ahh, redemption!

We spent the rest of the afternoon riding our bikes together. I couldn't help but notice that Taylor wasn't even utilizing the training wheels most of the time. Occasionally, he would tilt to one side, and when the training wheel hit the ground, he would shift his weight and rebalance himself back into the middle. I bit my tongue.

The next morning, I had barely come in from getting the Sunday paper off the driveway when I was greeted by a groggy Taylor. "Dad, I have a good idea. Can we ride our bikes again? Is that a good idea?"

It's funny how in parenting sometimes everything just

falls into place. "I have a better idea," I said. "What do you say we put on our tool belts, and you can take off just one of your training wheels first?" He was hooked.

No sooner had Taylor realized that he could ride perfectly fine with just one training wheel on, than he was asking me if he could take off the other. I handed him the wrench, and he took the other wheel off. One push and he rode away as if he'd never been afraid and had been riding all his life.

Despite his tough guy persona, Taylor had the kind of heart that rivaled the Tin Man's. When he rode back up our driveway, he stopped just in front of where I stood frozen, watching him in awe. Straddling his bike like a pro, he said, "You're the best dad for letting me use your tools."

Best dad? I thought. *Not yet . . . I'm still in training.*

Peter Balsino

Ultimate Dad

I recently turned fifty, which is young for a tree, midlife for an elephant, and ancient for a quarter miler, whose son now says, "Dad, I just can't run the quarter with you anymore unless I bring something to read."

Bill Cosby

It was a typical early April weekend in the western Massachusetts college town of Amherst. A few piles of snow still lingered in the yard as I threw the baseball around with my two sons in preparation for their annual baseball tryouts. My boys, Spencer and Jordan, had been playing baseball every spring and summer for the last six years. After a long baseball-free winter, it was almost time again for registration. We checked the cleats for size, tightened the webbing on the gloves, and began to dream of the season to come.

Little did I know of changes that lay in store for our family beginning the next day when Spencer walked in the house after school and announced, "There's been a slight change of plans. I'm playing Ultimate."

We were a little puzzled. "Ultimate what?" my wife inquired.

"Frisbee," he gleefully replied, and thus began our transformation from a baseball family to Frisbee fanatics. We had much to discover along the way about the game of Ultimate Frisbee, ourselves, and for me, "ultimately," about what it really means to be a dad.

I received a "crash course" in Ultimate Frisbee from our boys that spring. As I learned, Ultimate is an exciting and rapidly growing sport combining elements of football, basketball, and soccer, and requires tremendous speed, endurance, and agility.

Sounds like an exaggeration until you actually witness a game as I soon did one evening under the lights. I watched our highly ranked high school varsity boys Ultimate team take on one of their local rivals, the University of Massachusetts varsity team. Not often do you see high school kids playing against college kids!

I was amazed by the athleticism, skill, and grace I saw on the field, and was puzzled by the strange vocabulary of chants erupting spontaneously from the sideline. As my boys patiently explained, throws that start the play are called "pulls." The long leading throws to receivers running into open space are "puts." And the diving catches we witnessed all over the field are called "bids." I also got to see the mother of all Ultimate plays, a diving catch with the player flying horizontally to snare the flying disc out of thin air, the "layout."

But what really took me by surprise about Ultimate was the fact that, despite the intensity of the competition, no referees were anywhere in sight. The game was governed by adherence to the so-called "Spirit of the Game." Like golf and tennis, Ultimate was a game of honor and honesty. In fact, this self-regulation was an important part of why Ultimate appealed so much to my boys. When one player landed on top of another while both were diving for the disc, forcing a turnover, I watched in amazement as the two players calmly shared their versions of what happened, discussed it for a few seconds, and then agreed on how the issue would be resolved. All in the middle of a hotly contested point!

As we walked back to the car that night, I thought about this display of sportsmanship, and how a game in which this spirit of fairness was so pivotal could only be a good thing for the developing characters of my teenage boys.

I soon became as fascinated with Ultimate as Spencer and Jordan were and we began to spend our evenings in the yard with them patiently showing me the basic Ultimate techniques. As we worked on my forehand "flick," my catches, and curved throws, it became apparent that a role reversal had taken place with this game.

At forty-nine years of age, I was trying to learn *their* game, one suited for those much younger and much more physically fit. But I felt like I needed to share this game with them, to be able to fully appreciate their enthusiasm, which bordered on obsession. "I'll join the adult league!" I told them one night, surprising even myself. To be the best dad I could be, I needed to learn to play Ultimate!

And so with my boys coaching me, I continued my training in the lingo, rules, and throws of Ultimate in preparation for playing in the summer Ultimate League of Amherst.

When the evening of my first game finally arrived, I laced up my new cleats, grabbed my water bottle, and with some trepidation, headed off to join my new team. Even though I had registered for the "noncompetitive" adult division, I found players over forty were few and far between. As I took to the field, I was glad my boys were off at summer camp already so as not to witness my ineffective, haphazard, and I'm sure somewhat pathetic effort, sprinting in circles chasing a disc that always seemed just out of reach. Although I was constantly gasping for air, I did manage to catch the disc once or twice, and at the end of the night felt that I had done okay.

I had a little trouble walking the next day but proudly wrote a letter to both boys at camp detailing the difficulties I had on the field and asking for more tips. "I'll keep you posted," I wrote, promising to entertain them with the next week's episode of "Ultimate Dad."

I had almost recovered from the previous game and was warming up for my second when I began to feel a little tightness in my hamstrings. I did my best to stretch and went into the game only slightly more oriented as to the action than I was the week before. Fairly soon, I noticed my twenty-year-old defender was slacking off, probably because he was pretty sure I was not going to be much of a threat. I decided to sprint for an open area in the end zone and asked my increasingly tightening hamstrings for "high gear" in the hopes that someone would see me. Mr. Hayes, my boys' math teacher, spotted me cutting and floated the disc perfectly so that I could get to it as long as I continued at a dead sprint. At this point, I ignored the pain in my thighs, splashed through a puddle, and snagged the disc for my first goal. As I limped off of the field, I was smiling and thinking about my boys! "I did it!" I wrote to each of them later that night, hoping that in this continued role reversal they would be as proud of me as I have always been of them.

I always wanted my sons to follow my example. I never thought I'd be following theirs. Even though I will never be able to compete with Spencer and Jordan on the Ultimate Frisbee field, I am happy to be able to share their love and excitement for the game. I can now stand on the sideline shouting encouragement in their lingo, watching proudly as they diplomatically settle their own disputes on the field, fully appreciating their skill and the beauty of *our* game. And now that my hamstrings have fully healed, I have registered again for the upcoming season. Who knows? Maybe, if I'm lucky enough, one day I'll hear my boys shouting from the sideline, "Nice bid, Dad!"

Ted Diamond

"That's not what is meant by bonding, son."

First, a Father

Robert looked like a mountain man—big, with long hair and a bushy beard. He had gang-type tattoos around his wrist where a watchband would have rested had he been an office worker. He would look equally at home sitting on a rumbling Harley or in the backwoods wrestling a bear. Robert was not a man you would thump on the back of the head to see what happens.

He looked like a man who thrived on intimidation. Big across the shoulders and with muscular arms, he could have been a lumberjack. We were all surprised when he introduced himself as Robert, since our natural assumption was that he would proudly wear a "tag"—something like *Crusher* or *Brutus the Leg-Breaker*.

Robert was also a father of two boys in our church youth group and was eager to be a leader. As desperate as we were for adult volunteers, his desire to help sparked a fire of panic. Like all organizations that work with children, our church has a series of hurdles and verifications—mountains of forms—that adults must endure prior to being authorized. In this particular case, I was confident that the background check would be our nice way of denying Robert's participation without the current leaders being the bad guys.

"Oh, something didn't check in the background, Robert. You know how our investigators are," I was planning to say. "All it takes is some tiny little hiccup."

So there we sat, with me asking questions for the form, and he shyly answering. I suddenly realized that his eyes gave him away. His bulk and shaggy appearance flashed *threat*, but his eyes were warm and his voice gentle. He was a father wanting to help his two sons.

"And what do you do for a living?" I asked, my pencil poised.

"I buy drugs," he said.

"Oooookaaaaaaay," I said very slowly, as I wondered what the bored clerk in the back office would think as she processed my form. Well, at least he understood what the pastor had been teaching the boys about being trustworthy. He didn't lie.

I paused, not sure what to write or even say. That's when he laughed.

"I'm on the police force. I'm an undercover cop. Narc squad."

When you deal with the underworld, you don't arrive to work looking like a banker. His survival depended on making them believe in something he wasn't. I printed "Police Officer" in the little box and confidently forwarded the form knowing that he would add an interesting twist to our leadership team. Months later he was transferred to a more traditional police role and his hard edge softened considerably. Robert is a perfect example of why we need to slow down before jumping to conclusions.

David Wilkins

Dad's Gift

*Love only grows by sharing. You can only have
more for yourself by giving it away to others.*

Brian Tracy

Friday nights our 1960 household bustled with activity.
Mom and Dad often went bowling, and I liked to sleep
over with my girlfriends. At eighteen, my brother's weekends were filled with dates and school sports.

One winter Friday, both darkness and the temperature
were falling when Joe rushed madly through the house
searching for ready cash. His school's basketball team was in
an important play-off game that evening. A win would send
them to the state finals. Mom cleaned out her purse, and
Dad emptied his pockets. Even little sister shook her piggy
bank dry, but Joe was still short the price of admission.

"It's only the most important game of the season," he
moaned in typical teenage fashion.

Dad checked his watch. The bank was closed, and in
those days local grocery stores did not cash checks for more
than the amount of purchase. He shrugged his shoulders. "I
don't know what to tell you, son. We just don't have it."

Joe and his long face retired to the bedroom. No door slamming or yelling ensued. It wouldn't have helped. He sadly accepted the facts. He'd just have to miss the most important sports contest of his senior year.

Dad followed suit and went to his own bedroom. A few moments later he walked into the kitchen carrying an old cigar box. This was no ordinary cigar box. I recognized it as the box containing Dad's treasured coin collection. Mom and I looked at each other in amazement. For years Dad had saved every blackened nickel, every tarnished dime. He never spent pennies, but set them aside to later check the mint marks.

At least once a month, he and I dumped all those pennies and other coins onto the kitchen table and sorted them according to mint marks. D was for Denver, S for San Francisco, and no letter meant the penny was minted in Philadelphia. The blank ones were not considered valuable, but Dad thought D and S coins might someday be worth—well—a mint.

That Friday evening as game time neared, Dad didn't sort through coins, and he didn't scan the mint marks. He merely counted out the amount Joe needed for his ticket. Then he hurried to his son's bedroom and poured the coins into Joe's hand.

"I can't take this," my brother protested. "This is your coin collection. This is important to you."

"It's only money," said Dad with a grin. "I can get more. This basketball game will only happen once. Go on, now, before you miss the bus."

Joe gave Dad an awkward hug before shrugging into his coat and running out the back door, calling "Thank you" as it slammed. Once he was gone, Dad calmly scooped the remaining coins into the battered cigar box and returned it to its place on the dresser.

I was stunned, unable to believe Dad had willingly parted

with something of such value. How many hours of careful coin sorting had my brother stuffed into his coat pocket? We were not a rich family. I wondered how many years it would take my father to replace that pocketful of coins. Without a doubt, one or two of them were irreplaceable.

At age eleven I didn't really grasp the value of time or the worth of money. I didn't know much about sacrifice, but that night I learned a lesson about fatherhood that would last a lifetime.

That wintry Friday evening I got a good look at a father's heart, and I discovered it was made of love.

June Williams

2

I LOVE YOU, DAD . . . AND THANKS FOR EVERYTHING

Blessed is the man, indeed, who hears many gentle voices call him father!.

Lydia M. Child

"Look, Dad, I am tall enough to climb on the mantel!"

Heritage

Love and kindness are never wasted. They always make a difference. They bless the one who receives them, and they bless you, the giver.

Barbara De Angelis

For thirty-three years, *heritage* was just a word. It meant dead relatives I had never met.

My wife and I both grew up with fathers who earned their living in the construction trades. It was natural that we decided to build our own home. We were naïve enough to believe that meant something.

Linda's father lived fifty miles away and was fighting the later stages of cancer. Fortunately, my dad was an almost-constant working foreman at our job site. Even with an on- and off-site advisor, our building progress bore a resemblance to a turtle taking a bath.

Three months into our home-building program, Linda became pregnant with our second child. We were paying rent and making mortgage payments. We were spending virtually every night and every weekend at our new home while my mother cared for our son. Six months into this killer routine, both Linda and I caught the flu. We needed relief. We decided to spend money we didn't have to spare to hire Don Cronk to spackle our sheetrock.

Don did in less than a week what would have easily taken us six weeks to complete. We were delighted to have the work done so quickly, but we feared the inevitable invoice. When he handed us that dreaded reality, we were shocked. The bill was only a fraction of what we anticipated.

"Don, this can't be right," I said. He assured me that it was, but it was such a low number Linda and I pressed the issue.

"When I was down and out, your father was the only contractor who would give me work. I can't do anything for him, but I can give you this job at my cost," he said. My *heritage* suddenly hit me like a 250-pound linebacker. I hadn't done anything to deserve this good deed. My father earned the favor that I received.

I inherited a good name. That good name gave me a head start in life. I was the beneficiary of goodwill because my dad spent his life being an honest man who was in the habit of doing good deeds.

Today *heritage* is more than a word to me; it is a lifestyle. My children and grandchildren deserve an unbroken chain of goodwill. They deserve the same family legacy I took for granted until Don Cronk's putty knife scraped away my blindness.

Ed VanDeMark

The Good-Night Kiss

When our youngest child was a toddler, we had a horrible time getting him to sleep in his own bed. For whatever reason, long before morning had arrived in the master bedroom, Nathan was there.

Sometimes I woke up in time to see him crawl over me and slip beneath his father's arm. Seeing him there beside his father was enough to take my breath away, but we all knew it couldn't continue. No matter how many times Nathan promised to remain in his own bed all night, he just couldn't seem to follow the rules.

"Is there something wrong with your bed?" I asked, concerned that perhaps he perceived something frightening in his room.

He smiled up at me, wrinkled his nose, rolled his tongue around his mouth a few times, and then shook his head. "Nope," he replied, his blue eyes large and innocent.

Brightened by this information, I wondered if I could make his room more enjoyable by letting him help me rearrange it. He already loved his room—that much was obvious. He spent plenty of time in there during the day. But maybe a few more trucks, maybe a really cool night-light?

That afternoon Nathan and I went shopping. You never saw a happier little boy! He picked out a couple of trucks, a coloring book, and another stuffed animal. I figured we'd found the right combination of things this time, and when I tucked him into bed that night, I felt sure my little boy had passed over the threshold.

Wrong.

In the morning a tiny blond head was snuggled beneath my husband's arm again, his little body pointed at an awkward angle, feet planted firmly into my stomach. I shook my head and looked at the two of them. Then, unable to resist such an adorable photo opportunity, I tip-toed to the dresser for the camera.

Mothers are expected to teach their children certain things, like learning to break away from Mom.

The very next day Tom and I decided our son must be frightened and was obviously running to his comfort zone, which everyone knows is Momma.

So as any good mother would do, when bedtime rolled around that evening, I took my son by the hand. We walked into his bedroom and looked around. I pointed to everything in the room, asking quietly, "Do you like this? Do you want to take this out of your room?"

To each question, his eyes grew rounder and rounder and his head waggled back and forth. I could see he was beginning to worry where this was leading. Finally, kneeling at eye level with him, I asked if there were any "bad" things in his room. He did that adorable tongue-rolling thing and looked around the room anxiously, running one hand through the two blond curls at the base of his neck in a nervous gesture. Ah-ha, so there was some invisible danger. My heart sank. What could I do to make it all better?

Suddenly an idea formed. Smiling broadly, I asked if he'd like me to kick all those bad things out the door. Nathan's eyes grew enormous.

"Yap," he crowed.

I pushed my sleeves up and nodded seriously. "Okay. Where are they?"

He raced to his bed and pointed beneath it. I quickly dropped to my knees and pretended to grab a struggling and squealing "bad thing." I tucked it under one arm while I waited to find out where the other "bad things" were. Nathan pointed to the closet and I nabbed those "bad things" as they attempted to escape.

Nathan squealed in delight. Then he pointed behind the lamp. I stuck one hand under the shade and pulled the "bad things" out by the scruffs of their necks.

When we had them all rounded up, we marched to the front door and I drop-kicked the bundle of "bad things" from our house, yelling after them, "And don't come back!"

Nathan pointed one stubby finger out the door and yelled, "No come back!"

Satisfied, he looked up at me and smiled. I leaned down to ruffle that perfect little blond head but was a second too late. He was already racing down the hall.

A moment later, I stepped into his room. Hoping the charade had worked, I asked, "Are they all gone?"

"Yap," he said. Then he hugged my legs tightly and spun around the room one more time, his bright blue eyes scanning every nook and cranny. When he was satisfied, he looked up at me and spread his arms wide. "All gone," he crowed happily.

I smiled. "Good! Now you don't have to sleep with Momma anymore, do you?"

"Nope," he said, his mouth turned up into a precious grin. "You sleep here. Me sleep with Daddy!"

And as fast as his little legs could carry him, he raced to the door and disappeared.

By the time I reached the master bedroom, Nathan was already sliding beneath his father's arm. I stood in the hallway shadows and sighed. Just as I opened my mouth to tell Tom it was his turn to talk some logic into our son, I witnessed something that will forever be burned into my memory. Tom gently kissed the top of Nathan's tousled blond head. That was endearing enough to make my heart swell, but when Nathan closed his eyes contentedly and one chubby hand reached up to pat his father's head, an unexpected lump grew in my throat. When Tom tucked that very small boy beneath his chin and kissed that tiny palm, the lump in my throat grew humongous.

"Good night, son," Tom whispered.

"Night, Daddy," Nathan whispered back.

"Momma coming to bed?" Tom mumbled.

"Nope," Nathan mumbled back.

Within seconds only the sound of their even breathing filled the room. Both were oblivious to the woman in the doorway, tears streaming down her face, the woman who loved them both enough to realize this was not about her at all. It was about a father and his son and their need to be together.

Helen Kay Polaski

The Big Decision

As human beings, our greatness lies not so much in being able to remake the world . . . as in being able to remake ourselves.

Gandhi

All year long my son Alec had been dreaming about getting a bike. He'd learned to ride the year before and asked me and his mom to get him a bicycle for his birthday. He looked at hundreds of bikes over the next few months, trying to decide which one he wanted, and one day while we were looking in a store, Alec stopped in front of a shiny blue bicycle and said, "Dad, that's the one I'd like for my birthday."

I'd taught my son the value of saving for what he wanted. A bike was an expensive item at that time in our lives. My wife and I were busy working and paying bills and taking care of our family. Trying to feed and clothe four children wasn't easy, but we were keeping our heads above water. The only thing we didn't have money for was a brand-new bike. Telling my son this was a hard thing to do, but he came up with his own solution.

"I've been saving my allowance," he told me. "What if I save for the rest of the year? I'd have enough money saved to pay for half the bike I want by my birthday."

This sounded like a solution King Solomon would have been proud of. I was proud of my son, too. He was showing a great deal of maturity and responsibility for his age. Little did I know that this was just the beginning of how he would come to surprise me that year.

Alec had to sacrifice to save for his birthday bike. While his siblings spent their money on special clothing, movies, and other fun things, Alec carefully counted out his monthly allowance and put it into his piggy bank. I saw in his eyes the temptation to spend it whenever he watched the others buying things, but Alec would go back to the store that had his birthday bike and look through the window. Then he'd nod as if he'd made a decision and the money in his bank would remain untouched for another month.

This went on month after month until his birthday was just around the corner. Alec counted and recounted the money in his piggy bank almost every night. He'd race over to the store where his birthday bicycle was waiting. He'd glance at the price tag, do some quick mental calculations, and smile when he knew he'd make it to the halfway mark by his birthday. It was just a matter of weeks. The bike was as good as his.

Then one of those unplanned events that life is full of occurred. Our car developed a crack in the transmission. The mechanic told me that it would cost over a thousand dollars to repair. There was no way we could afford that, but the car was vital to my wife and me getting to our jobs. The mechanic offered to replace it with a used transmission for a slightly lower price. I went home and sat down at the kitchen table and tried to figure out how we were going to afford it.

By cutting out every expense we could, it looked like we would just be able to do it. We would have no money left for extras, including paying for even half of the cost of a new bike. I felt terrible at the thought of having to tell Alec that all his hard work would not get him the bike he deserved, but there was nothing else I could do.

"I'm sorry we won't be able to buy you a brand-new bike," I told him later that night. "Things are stretched too tight, and the repairs on the car will take a lot of money."

Alec nodded, trying not to look at me. His voice shook when he spoke. "I understand, Dad. The car needs to be fixed. Maybe next year."

"Hey," I said, trying to come up with my own brilliant solution. "Maybe we can get you a used bike. We saw some pretty cool ones in the bicycle shop when we first looked for your birthday bike."

Alec's face grew brighter. "I do have enough money saved for a used bike."

"Sure," I said, "And I can buy some paint and we can make it blue just like the one you wanted. At least you'll be able to ride your own bike until we can afford to get you a new one."

Alec got his piggy bank down from its shelf and began to count his money. I saw the joy in his face at the thought of a bike for his birthday. Then he stopped counting. Alec sat there for the longest time. Then he scooped up all of the money he had saved for more than half a year.

"Dad," he said slowly, "I want you to take this money to help pay for the car."

I stood there not knowing what to say. Alec was smiling, but I couldn't believe he wanted to do this. "Alec, you've saved for so long for your birthday bike."

Alec nodded. "I wanted the bike, but I wanted it so I could ride to school and to my friends' houses. You drive me to school in the car, and to visit my friends, and we need the car so you and Mom can get to work to keep taking care of us. Somehow that seems more important right now than a bicycle."

"Are you sure?"

Alec nodded. Then he smiled again and said, "Can I ask one favor?"

"Sure. What is it?"

"Well, since I'm sort of helping out with the car, can I borrow it sometime when I'm older and get a driver's license?"

I laughed and gave him a hug. "You got a deal."

John P. Buentello

[AUTHOR'S NOTE: *Alec didn't have to wait until he was old enough to borrow the car, because the following year the whole family saved and surprised him with a bike on his birthday.*]

Saved

Life is a sum of all your choices.

Albert Camus

I can't say I much liked my father while I was growing up. Typical stuff bothered me—overworked dad, factory job, mom at home with three babies. I was the middle one. We lived in Brooklyn, New York, near my dad's family. He didn't understand me and couldn't possibly grasp the sixties. Many factors defined his life: coming from an immigrant family, working hard, joining the Army, working hard, marrying his Army sweetheart, working hard, coming home and having babies, and working hard all the while. "Get a job," I heard from him from the time I was fourteen years old.

I must say, in my mom's later years, after Dad had died, I was very surprised to hear her stories of their life before kids—sneaking off together during the war when they were both stationed in England, hopping a train to Scotland, spending a weekend together against all regulations; living in New York City and going out dancing every weekend; generally having the time of their lives.

This was not the dad I knew. "No, you can't go to another movie. We can't afford that." That's the dad I knew.

I knew strict, angry, distant, tired. I knew his volunteering to walk to work during the worst snowstorms, leaving us home with Mom. I knew special, better food for Dad. I knew Mom keeping us kids in line so as not to upset him. I knew his anger when we went too far. "I'll give you something to cry about." That's the dad I knew.

He gave me $100 when I moved out of the house at age eighteen to seek my fortune.

I visited him regularly, my growing family in tow. My wife and kids loved him, but they loved my mom more easily. I cared for Dad but did not know how to love him. I don't know if we would have even stayed in touch had it not been for Mom. Luckily, she kept the wheels greased, and our family stayed connected; siblings and parents and the next generation of kids got to know one another because Mom kept it all happening.

It was at a family gathering that I first noticed: Dad's jaw was a little slack, his speech a little slurred. I mentioned it to Mom. Soon after this, he fell. I told Mom to take it seriously. She did and sought medical attention for Dad.

The doctors promised his brain tumor was operable, not malignant, and would be no big deal to fix. Dad was stoic. Mom was scared. I tried to get Dad to talk about some important things: his will, money, wishes for burial. He refused. Same old dad. He'd be in charge till the end.

Then things went wrong. He survived the surgery, just barely. He spent weeks in the hospital, surgery after surgery, in and out of consciousness. He'd get better one week, go into rehab, and crash the next week, then he'd be back to the hospital. Mom was always at his side.

I drove the three hours from my house to the hospital weekly, sometimes more. My family came often. Even the little ones sat at his hospital bed. On a particularly bad day, my six-year-old daughter was with him, and he faded back in time, thinking he was with his own daughter. He softened visibly and held her hands. "I love you."

"I love you, too, Grandpa."

I saw for the first time the loving father he had probably always been, hidden behind his hard work and worry.

I began softening, too.

On Christmas Eve, my mother leaned over to her husband and said, "It's okay to leave, Ted." She loved him and didn't want him to suffer anymore. On Christmas morning we got the call. "Dad is gone." I softened still more, but not enough to cry as my wife and kids did, so easily and authentically.

We moved through the funeral. Then I had to start asking my mom the hard questions: "Where's his will?" "Do you have money, Ma?" "Was there life insurance?" She knew virtually nothing. He was truly old school. Even though my mother was an Army nurse and an officer to boot, even though she worked in methadone clinics in the darkest parts of New York City, even though she reared three babies mostly by herself, she had never handled the checkbook, didn't know about insurance, and now she was left in the dark after Dad died.

The softening I felt for dad during those difficult months faded and my anger returned. *Stubborn, as always*, I thought. *Too proud for his own good.* My wife and I began to think about how we could help support Mom. She would get his Social Security. But it wasn't enough to live on. She was only seventy-four.

I began to feel what he must have *always* felt: scared for the well-being of those he loved. I began to despair. We were living close to the edge, as were both my siblings. No one had extra money.

And then in cleaning out yet another box of his personal items—cuff links, tie tacks, company awards, old can openers, souvenirs of places he'd visited—I found a safety deposit box key. "Mom, where's the safety deposit box Dad has?" She had never heard of it.

Luckily, this small town had just two banks. We got it right on the first try and went with death certificate and key to open the safety deposit box. "Did you all have family heirlooms he might have put away?"

"No," Mom said. "It's probably just papers from work. He always saved everything from work."

The box did contain papers from work, but not the kind she'd expected. My dad had diligently bought stock in the company he had worked for, first as a laborer, then as a foreman, and finally as a vice president, one stock certificate at a time.

Every movie we didn't go to, every dress Mom didn't get, the big red fire engine I wanted and didn't get was in that box. I can't even imagine what Dad had wanted and didn't get that went straight into that box.

That's when I cried and softened for good.

"Your dad was so peaceful when he was dying. I didn't know why it was easy for him. Now I do. He promised to take care of me forever, and he has kept his promise," Mom said.

Yes, he had. And the promise he made to me, that I never really heard, was the promise of my becoming a good man. I now have a small pile of stocks, too. They just happen to be with a stockbroker, not in a small metal box.

Ted Slawski

Love's Lesson

My childhood was filled with hunting, camping, and fishing trips. My parents did not have much money, but they gave us a far better currency—their time. One Thanksgiving I watched my mom and dad cook together. As my father worked beside my mother, my heart filled with love and admiration. I just wanted to say, "I love you, Dad." Throughout the day, I tried to speak those difficult words "I lov . . ." But I could not utter the words.

Thanksgiving dinner came and went. I laid on my bed, stuffed like the turkey that had sat on the table a short time ago. What a great time we'd had, family time and wonderful food. My only regret is that I had not spoken those three difficult words—I love you.

I awoke early the next day. Fall had given way to wintry weather, and a fresh blanket of snow lay gently upon the mountains. My father had decided to go deer hunting with my brothers. I went skiing.

After an invigorating day on the slopes, I returned home. The house was cold and still. I called out, but no one answered. Usually, Mom was always busy in the kitchen preparing one meal or another. The quietness was broken by the sudden shrill ring of the telephone.

"Your father has been shot in a hunting accident," said a neighbor from the farm house nearby. "He's in surgery and not expected to live."

At that moment my failure to say "I love you" pushed down on me like the weight of the fallen sky. The neighbor came over and quickly drove me to the hospital.

Trembling, I entered the intensive care unit. My father lay motionless on a hospital bed. Tubes sprouted from every part of his body. He could not breathe on his own. He was the rock in my life. He had always been there for me. When I learned to drive he coached me, when I wanted to drop out of college he encouraged me to keep going and not give up. Now he lay lifeless, totally dependent on machines.

Soon, I discovered the details of the accident. A high-powered rifle bullet had hit him in the chest and exited under his arm. The bullet took out four ribs and a third of his lung.

Bone fragments and metal chips now rested within a quarter inch of his heart. All I could think was that he was slipping into eternity without hearing those words "I love you." Afraid to leave him, I sobbed uncontrollably as I clung to his bedside.

"It's time to go," said the critical care nurse. "The next twenty-four hours will be critical."

I returned home heavy hearted. My mother called my sister and two brothers and me together. For the first time we prayed as a family. Mom asked me to pray that God would spare Dad's life. All I could think of was that I wanted just one more chance to express my love to my father. After praying, we looked one another in the eyes and said those forbidden words—"I love you."

At that moment my fear of expressing those words was broken. I knew that our family would never be the same. But would it be too late for my father?

None of us got much sleep that night. I expected the phone to ring at any moment—a call to announce that my father had slipped into eternity. Early in the morning the phone did ring. My heart almost stopped beating.

"This is the hospital," said a nurse. "We just wanted your family to know that your father has made a miraculous recovery. He is awake and asking for all of you."

"Thank you, dear God, for giving me another chance," I uttered as I hung up the phone.

That morning we gathered around my father's bedside. His first words to us were "I love you." I was able to tell him that I loved him, too.

By the time Dad was released from the hospital it was almost Christmas. The joy of his return was soon dampened by the financial reality of no health insurance and a $25,000 medical bill. Needless to say, we did not exchange presents that year. Instead, we sat Dad next to the Christmas tree on Christmas morning and covered him with bows. Having him alive and with us to love was the best present we could ever have. I wrapped my arms around my father and looked into his eyes and said, "I love you."

Dennis Hixson

What's in a Name?

Modeling may not only be the best way to teach; it may be the only way to teach.

Albert Schweitzer

It had been a long, brutal day on the sales floor for young Brent. He'd had his share of "ups"—what retail salespeople say when it's their turn with the next customer—and more than his share of downs. And now he was in danger of being shut out for the day.

He hadn't been shut out in a long time. Even in his early days with the company, he could always sell something to someone. That's why he became assistant manager so quickly. He was a good salesman. A natural. And he had a knack for turning new customers into repeat customers.

But on this day, there were no customers. At least none who wanted to buy. Plenty of customers wanted to look, and he spent a lot of time with each one. But he could never close the deal. This, of course, exposed him to some good-natured ridicule from his associates, who took not-so-secret delight in seeing the sales prodigy get his comeuppance.

Brent had more at stake here than just professional pride and reputation, however. Brent was a new father. He and his wife, Kay, had decided that she would be a full-time mom, which meant he would financially support the family. When he did well on the sales floor, finances weren't a problem. But when he struggled to make sales, the whole family struggled.

And on this day, he was struggling.

Toward the end of the day, a man came in to buy a suit. This was potentially a good sale, the kind that can turn a bad day into a good one—just like that. Brent worked hard to make the sale. The man tried on several suits. Brent carefully explained the materials, the craftsmanship, and why these suits, although expensive, were such a good buy.

The man hesitated. Brent knew all too well the look he saw in his eyes—the look of a customer about to walk out the door empty-handed—and he was tempted to use some of the tricks he had learned to pressure people into making a purchase. But he had long since decided that high pressure salesmanship wasn't the way he wanted to do business. So when it became clear that the man was going to leave to do a little comparison shopping, Brent handed him his business card and invited him to return after he'd had a chance to look around.

The man looked at Brent's card, then took a long look at Brent.

"So you're Brent's boy," the man said, referring to the the card that identified him as Brent Jr.

"Do you know my dad?" Brent asked.

"Sure do," the man said. They chatted for a moment, establishing the link between father and son. Then the man said, "Your dad's a good man. If you're anything like him . . . well, tell me again about that suit."

Brent made the sale. But that wasn't why he called his

father that night to recount the story. "I just wanted to thank you," he said, "for giving me a name I can be proud of."

Tears were in Brent Sr.'s eyes as he hung up the phone, and gratitude in his heart that for all of the dumb things he had done in his life—and we all do them, don't we?—he hadn't done anything dumb enough to dishonor the name he shared with his son.

Joseph Walker

Three Little Words

As the four of us stood in my father's living room, his brand-new bride, Claudia, smiled and reached out her arms. "Before Don and Bonnie go," she said, "how about all of us hug, kiss, and say, 'I love you'?"

I froze. I stared at her, at my wife, Bonnie, at my eighty-three-year-old father, Oliver. Would he actually say those three little words—to me?

You see, my father and I had seen very little of each other over the years. His first wife, my mother, Fern, nearly died when I was born. Then when my younger brother, Dean, was born three years later, she collapsed completely. After being hospitalized for many years, she suffered a fatal heart attack. So we boys were brought up mostly by our two grandmothers.

Oliver was a proud, outgoing father at first. But the years of my mother's illness wore on him, especially after we boys went to northern Wisconsin to live with Granny Hanson. For all we knew, he might have blamed us for our mother's illness and eventual death. After that, we only got to see him on his once-a-year vacations.

Then when I was thirteen, our father married again, to a young widow with a daughter just my age. "We'll all be one big happy family," Oliver announced, "at our new home out in California. You boys and I will be together at last. Won't that be wonderful?"

But Dean and I had been too many years without our father, and we hungered for his complete attention, for him to hug us and say, "I love you." Our new stepsister competed just as vigorously for her mother's love. So no matter how hard Oliver and his new wife, Jean, tried, our newly "blended" family refused to blend—especially me. It didn't seem fair to have to share my dad after so many years of missing him. Finally, my father gave up and sent me 2,000 miles away to live again with Granny Hanson.

When I was fifteen, my beloved grandmother died. After that, I lived with various relatives. Finally, at sixteen I missed my father so much I worked all summer on a farm, saved every penny, and took a one-way trip out West. How I looked forward to our reunion.

But my father and his wife didn't. Everything had been peaceful with me out of the way, and my stepmother didn't want to risk having trouble again. So instead of welcoming me home, Dad sent me to the local YMCA. I stayed there, working on local farms, until the day I turned seventeen. Then, convinced there was no hope for me to ever be with my father again, I joined the Army.

Struck by a mortar in Korea, I spent several years in hospitals in Japan and the States. When I had recovered enough, I enrolled in college in Illinois. Eventually I graduated, started seminary, and met and married Bonnie. My dad did come from California for the wedding—the first time I'd seen him in eight years. But we had no time for catching up and sharing. He stayed with relatives and soon left for California again.

After my stepmother died, Oliver married again. By this time Bonnie and I had three little boys and wanted him to meet them, so we traveled to California. My new stepmother, Rosalie, a warm, loving person and talented artist, tried to make us welcome. But with my father we still seemed to be company, not family. He was even reserved with his young grandsons. When they ran to hug him, he stopped them with, "Men don't hug; they shake hands." Would I never hear from him those three little words I'd been waiting to hear all my life?

Eventually we moved to California ourselves, close enough to visit occasionally. By now, after years of being a stock accountant, entrepreneur, and jazz clarinetist, my father had retired from his "day jobs"—but was more active in music than ever. Then Rosalie began ailing and finally passed away. By now Dad was eighty-three and in great health. My own sons were grown, and I was thrilled at the fine young men they had become. Yet after all these years, I doubted that my own dad and I would ever have that warm father-son relationship my sons and I have.

But I hadn't counted on Claudia. A widow herself and professional artist, she had helped care for Rosalie during her lingering illness. After Rosalie died, Claudia and Oliver discovered that they had developed a great fondness for each other. Although they hesitated, I encouraged them to get married. In fact, as a pastor myself, I offered to marry them!

Now the joyful wedding party was over, with just the four of us left. "Let's all hug, kiss, and say, 'I love you,'" the new bride had suggested. Bonnie and I, of course, were more than willing. But what about Dad?

At first he looked shocked. Then suddenly he glowed. Reaching out trembling arms, he said, "I love you" to each one of us individually. Including me! And he hugged and kissed me for the first time in over forty years!

My father lived for ten more years, doing three gigs a week, even at ninety-three. In fact, Bonnie and I played in one of his bands. He got to know our sons and grandsons and became not just a photo but part of the family. Those three little words had unlocked a lifetime of waiting love, and we had some wonderful times together during his remaining years.

Oh, how thankful I am for the power of those three little words, and I say them to my own sons as often as possible.

"I love you." And I mean it!

Don J. Hanson
As told to Bonnie Compton Hanson

The Kind of Man a Boy Needs

I was three years old when my father ran away. He left, unexpectedly, vanished like a wisp of smoke, and I wasn't even sure who it was who had stepped out of my life. I remember little about my father. My mother refused to discuss him. She could scarcely bring herself to speak his name. When he left, he never returned. It was as if he had simply disappeared from the face of the earth.

My mother and I lived in a small mill town in northern California. It was a town of chuckholed streets, junglelike lawns, and houses as bleak as a hundred-year-old ghost town. Unemployment was endemic there. What I remember most vividly about those days was the embarrassment. I had no father. He had let us down. He had failed to do what a man was supposed to do if he was to call himself a man: work hard, pay his debts, and stand by his family forever.

The numbers attached to the years slowly changed. During that time my mother and I never went anywhere. We enjoyed no vacations or weekend outings, no movies. We had little money in our house for such things. Then one day, everything changed. A man fell from the sky and landed at our dinner table. I was ten years old, but I remember it as though it were yesterday.

That winter day began brittle with cold. Plates of ice covered the puddles. I was in bed when I heard a car pull into the driveway. I peeked out the window and saw a blue Chevy pickup, motor idling, vapors rising in the gelid air. A strange man sat behind the wheel, looking big and full of purpose. Mom told me he was coming—my new stepfather. He had married my mother only a week before in Nevada. I was choked with excitement. *What would he think of me?* My hair wasn't combed and I hadn't brushed my teeth. I was taken with a terrible idea: what if he had seen me already? What if he thought, *This kid will never make a decent son. A boy should be stronger and taller.*

My mother called from the living room. I stuffed my shirttail into my pants, hollered, "Yeah?" and straightened up erect, prepared to make the best manly impression possible. Then I opened my bedroom door and strode into the living room. There, in the flesh, was the father I had dreamed of in a thousand forms since I'd realized that other boys had a second parent, a parent who knew men's stuff and could pass it down to them.

He introduced himself. His name was Ernie—Ernest McKenzie. His voice was rough, yet caressing, like the lick of a tomcat's tongue. He had bare-looking green eyes, a gap between his top teeth, and hair as black as wrought iron that was combed with force off his forehead. He offered his hand and I shook it. His grip was meaty, muscular. He was, as I knew from a boy's curiosity and observation, unusually strong.

"How's the fishing around here?" he asked.

I had no idea. I had never caught a fish in my life.

"I don't know," I murmured, hardly daring to raise my eyes to his.

He fixed a cigarette on his bottom lip, snapped a little

no-nonsense stainless steel lighter under it, and returned
the lighter to the chest pocket of his shirt. The smoke rose
up the right side of his face, so he narrowed that eye.

"Well, we're just gonna have to find out," he said, and
tipped me a wink.

A thrill rippled through me in that wink. It put the two
of us in cahoots; it made us secret allies in a manly way.
After my mother finished showing Ernie around our small
house, he pulled me aside and said, "Say, I got a great idea.
How would you like to go fishing tomorrow?"

"S-sure," I stammered. "But . . ."

"No buts about it," he said. "I'll wake you in the morning." Then he handed me a half dollar and asked me if I
would run to the store.

Would I run to the store? I would have circled the globe
if he had requested it! I was falling all over myself getting
out the door. I was just pulling out of the driveway on my
bicycle when Ernie hollered, "Get yourself a candy bar, too."

The man is a god, I remember thinking as I pedaled down
the block toward the corner store.

As Ernie promised, he woke me early the next morning
to go fishing. Our destination was the Eel River. It dipped
out of the mountains to the east and slid past our small
town. Ernie assured me trout were in the river, big speckled trout with bellies as red as cherry candy.

By the time we reached the river, the sun was up. Our
fishing spot was downstream from a small waterfall. The
rock reef was about two feet under the water, so the whole
river rose into one wave, shook itself into spray, then fell
back and turned blue. Ernie added sinkers and hooks to
our lines. Then he threaded worms onto the hooks. A fish
jumped from the blue water, flashing like quicksilver.

"See right there?" He pointed to the place where the
trout had jumped. "Wow! She was a big one."

Ernie always called things *she*, but I couldn't tell how he knew. He would say, "I guess she'll be a hot one today," or "It looks like she'll rain." Or when we were fishing, "Just skim the worm across the water and watch her jump."

I drew back and made my cast.

"Did I get her in the right spot?" I asked.

"Just right," Ernie said.

The line tightened and the current carried the worm into sight at the end of the pool. I could feel the sinkers tap-tapping on the rocks. Suddenly, the tip of my pole dipped and the line straightened, taut as a wire. I jerked and reeled in quick. On the end of my line was a ten-inch speckled trout. My hands were shaking, but finally I managed to grab the fish and shout to Ernie: "Look! I got one!"

"Hey, that's a beauty," he said, launching a terrific smile. "And it's the first catch of the day. You're turning out to be quite a fisherman."

I preened inwardly, murmuring my thanks. Already I liked everything about Ernie. I thought to myself he was the kind of man a boy needs around when he's growing up. If I was going to call any man my father, he would be a good man to choose.

Tim Martin

"I'm glad Mom married you, Dad.
You're a stepfather in the right direction."

Thanks to the Dragon

I am a recently divorced dad with a fourteen-year-old son. As with most dads in my position, I don't see my son as often as I'd like to. My father died when I was young and I have few memories of him. As a result, my relationship with my son is the most important thing to me; however, with teenagers being what they are, I don't always know what's going on inside my son's head.

When Alex was about five years old, we lived briefly in California. His mother was in the Air Force, and this was her first assignment. I worked a couple of part-time jobs and, as a result, had some time off during the week. I often took him to a park we dubbed the "Dragon Park" because there was a concrete dragon character at the entrance.

In addition to the dragon (which all the kids played on), the park had a vast playground area with lots of playground equipment to climb on, through, around, and more. Alex always looked forward to going to the park and hated when it was time to leave.

These days, I see my son twice during the week and then on the weekend. One weekend, he told me about a project he had in his English class. He was to write about a place or time in his life that was important to him and how he felt about it. The feeling could be positive or negative.

"So what did you decide to write about?" I asked.

"I wanted to write about the Dragon Park, Dad," was his reply.

I had thought he would've chosen someplace that we had traveled to, like Japan or Hawaii, and asked him why he chose the Dragon Park.

"These were the times when I felt the closest to you," he answered. It was all I could do to hold back the tears until after I got back to my apartment.

When I got home, I went through the boxes of photos that I had taken of him over the years. I came across one of him with a big smile on his face sitting on that dragon. I took it to a photo shop, had it enlarged, and bought a frame for it.

That following Thursday, I went to see him. As he opened the door, I handed him a wrapped package.

"What's this?" he asked.

"Go ahead and open it," I said.

He ripped off the paper and held the framed picture in his hand. He looked up at me without saying anything.

"Those were some of my favorite times together, too, son." At that point, he wrapped his arms around me and gave me a big bear hug.

With everything involved with being an adolescent, going to Dragon Park with me was the memory he drew upon for his assignment. I used to worry about what memories he'd have of me after I'm gone, but not any more.

Dave Quist

Grass-Cutting Days

*If the only prayer you ever say in your entire life
is "thank you," it will be enough.*

Meister Eckhart

The pastor called me to come forward. I walked to the
pulpit confident and proud. I looked out at my family.
Some wore somber expressions. Others had faces still
damp with tears. I gazed down at the shiny black coffin
crowned with yellow flowers. My father was gone. It was
my turn to pay tribute to the man who had taught me so
much. How do you sum up a lifetime in ten minutes?

I flashed to Dad holding the handlebar and jogging
alongside my bike until I felt ready to ride on my own. I
saw him pulling up to my broken-down car at night in a
rough part of town. He did a quick fix and trailed me
home. I thought of the hug we shared at my wedding.

Then I started talking about a special moment.

Dad was always full of advice, but one of the biggest
lessons he taught me one summer was about having a
strong work ethic. When my brother and I were growing
up, we mowed yards during the summer to earn pocket

change. Dad was our salesman. He pitched our service to neighbors and offered a price they could not refuse. My brother and I received $10 per yard. Some yards were a half acre. I later discovered our friends charged $20 or more for the same amount of work.

Every time we headed out to mow lawns, Dad was there to watch. I used to wonder why he came with us. He stood supervising our work in the sticky Florida heat when he could have been inside relaxing with air-conditioning and an icy drink.

One day, we were cutting our next-door neighbor's yard. She always waited until the grass was knee-high before she called us to mow her lawn. To make matters worse, we had an old lawn mower that kept cutting off as we plowed through her backyard jungle. This particular afternoon, I was finishing up and was tired and sweaty. I pictured the tall glass of Kool-Aid I would gulp in a minute to cool down.

I was just about to cut off the lawn mower when I saw Dad pointing to one lone blade. I thought about the chump change I was getting paid for cutting grass so high it almost broke the mower. I ignored him and kept walking. Dad called me and yelled, "You missed a piece." I frowned, hoping he would let me slide and go home. He kept pointing.

Beat and deflated, I went back to cut that piece of grass. I mumbled to myself, "That one piece isn't hurting anyone. Why won't he just let it go?"

But when I reached adulthood, I understood his message: when you're running a business, the work you do says a great deal about yourself. If you want to be seen as an entrepreneur with integrity, you must deliver a quality product. That single blade of uncut grass meant the job was not done.

Other neighbors took notice of the good work we did,

and we soon garnered more business. We started out with one client, but by the end of the summer we had five, which was all we cared to handle because we wanted time to enjoy our summer break from school.

The lesson my dad taught me stayed with me: be professional. If you say you are going to perform a job at a certain time, keep your word. Give your customers the kind of service you would like to receive. It shows how sincere you are and how much pride you take in your work.

Before I knew it, my tribute was over. I saw my wife jump to her feet in an ovation. The pastor embraced me. People rushed to shake my hand. Though Dad's body lay inside the coffin, I felt his spirit there. I pictured him standing in the sanctuary, wearing the white T-shirt and blue shorts he did on grass-cutting days, always there for me and always proud.

Patrick Lyons

"Before I mow the grass I'd like to quote from section four, paragraph C of the state child labor code."

The Power of a Son's Kiss

He's well into his teenage years, yet my son still kisses me good night. I'm sure going to miss it when he stops. In truth, he stopped once a few years ago when he announced he was "a little too old for this," but changed his mind after we had a father and son talk. I've always known the spoken word can deliver a powerful message, but as I learned that night, sometimes the message needn't be voiced at all. And sometimes the greatest lessons learned are taught to us unknowingly by our children. One of the things we talked about that night was an old friend of mine.

We were going camping for the weekend. When I stopped to pick up my friend, he and his father were working together on a classic car restoration. Grabbing his gear and before leaving he said, "See you on Sunday, Pop," and without hesitation, gave his father a kiss. So many years have gone by since then, yet the memory of that moment remains with me—a lasting impression of the love my friend had for his father and demonstrated through the power of a kiss.

My son and I talked about my father, too. I wish I could

kiss Dad once more, but he passed away some years ago. We didn't kiss as grown men until I was well into adulthood. When I began to kiss him again it was on special occasions—holidays, family gatherings—times when I could do so with neither of us feeling embarrassed or uncomfortable. It was a wonderful feeling to express my love for him in such a way, and I knew he felt so, too. Not since my childhood had kissing served as a routine declaration of affection between us, but once resumed, we both had come to expect it. On the night he died and again one last time before he was laid to rest, I tenderly kissed him and whispered, "I love you." This is what I told my son— not with intent to embarrass him into continuing our nightly ritual, but instead to share with him a small piece of the love I had for my father and how much he had meant to me. He listened, and when I was through, he kissed me. We haven't missed a night since.

Many times I have wondered if our nightly ritual was about to reach its untimely demise, the consequence of some offense committed by my firstborn. Having duly expressed my dissatisfaction with something my son has said or done, the ensuing verbal sparing commences. He unknowingly exposes his vulnerability when he says things in anger, part of his full-speed quest toward manhood. Despite any ill feelings that might remain between us as the day draws to a close, we never allow such emotions to interfere with our nightly kiss. When my son is ready for bed, he finds me. When I see him, any anger I experienced earlier quietly disappears. He stands before me, not quite a man but for the moment, my little boy. He seeks my reassurance that we are okay and that I still love him. I give a comforting hug, the nightly kiss, and the reaffirmation that regardless of his transgressions, my love remains unconditional, eternal. As he heads off to bed I bask in the glow of fatherly love and the reassurance that he still needs me. Once again our private world has been made right, if but for one more night.

I hope my son never feels uncomfortable kissing me, but if he ever does, I'll understand. Perhaps one day he'll be blessed with children of his own and then he, too, will come to know the wonder and glory of fatherhood and the power of his child's kiss.

Stephen Wayne

Sharing Love

Family isn't about whose blood you have. It's about who you care about.

Trey Parker and Matt Stone

When my son, David, was six, he got the idea that he could call heaven on his toy antique telephone. He'd pick up the earpiece and pretend to call his father, who died in a car accident when David was three, and have a one-sided, cheerful conversation about his toys, books, and Mommy.

One day he introduced a new topic. "Hi, Daddy, this is David. We met this guy, and his name is Jeff. He's really nice," he said. Jeff was the new man in our lives. We'd met through mutual friends, and he seemed so perfect for me and David that I wondered if I'd invented him. David was thrilled to have someone new to play with and talk to. He loved to sit on Jeff's lap and discuss Winnie the Pooh or show him Lego creations.

One afternoon Jeff stopped at our house while David was napping after morning kindergarten. David woke from his nap and came to the door of the living room.

When he saw Jeff and me hugging, he stopped abruptly, his big brown eyes startled. Then he turned and raced into the bathroom, slammed the door, locked it, and began to wail with huge heart-wrenching sobs.

I ran to the bathroom door. "David, will you let me in?" I asked softly. Sobs were the answer.

"David, I love you. Would you like me to rock you?" I asked quietly. The door unlocked but did not open. The sobs continued.

Slowly I opened the door. The little brown-haired boy wouldn't look up, and his body was rigid.

I led him to the big gold rocker recliner in the living room. His sobs continued, quieter now, as I picked him up, sat in the rocker, and began to rock. He'd lost his dad. Now he felt he was losing his mom, too, to that big man named Jeff.

This was not a time for talking. It was a time for primitive rocking. So I rocked and rocked. And I didn't talk and I didn't sing. I just held tight and rocked. And I thought of all the times his father had rocked him in this chair, all the times I had nursed him there, and all the times we still squeezed together there for bedtime stories.

What could I say that would help? Could I help him understand that my loving Jeff did not mean loving him less? How could I help him understand I was not abandoning him, that he was not losing me, too?

I closed my eyes as the crying continued. *Please help me know what to say, what to do,* I prayed.

Suddenly an image of candles being lit came into my mind.

I whispered, "Do you want to hear a story about candles?" The little head nodded sharply but did not look up.

"Love is like a candle's flame. If you share your candle's light, you just get more light. If you share your love, you get more love." *This is too abstract,* I fumed inwardly.

"Do you want to see how the candles' love works?" I asked. The head nodded.

We located the birthday candles and matches in the kitchen and turned out the light. Then we sat by the kitchen table, facing each other, knees touching.

I lit a birthday candle and handed it to him. His eyes were alert but sad. "Here's the little boy candle," I said. "He has love." I lit my candle from his. "Here's the mommy candle. He shares his love with the mommy candle. Now they both have love.

"Let's put your candle and my candle together," I suggested. We did, and the combined flame flickered high. "Wow, they have lots of love together," I said.

As if on cue, Jeff, who had stepped into the office to give us privacy, slipped into the kitchen and lifted David onto his lap.

I lit a third candle and handed it to Jeff. "Here's the friend candle. The mommy candle shares some love with the friend candle. But look, she still has all her love left. . . . Let's put all the candles together," I said.

We touched our three candles together. The flame rose, casting a soft light on the kitchen. "Wow, look what a big love we make when we all share love together," I said.

Jeff and I looked at each other over David's head. Was it time to personalize the message? we asked each other's eyes.

"David," Jeff said quietly, daring to say the words I couldn't yet. "Do you know who these candles are? That's David and Mommy and Jeff." We touched our flames together and the flame rose high again.

"We need another candle," David said in a little voice. "Daddy."

I lit another candle and held it about two feet away. "Here's the daddy candle. He loves us and we love him. But we can't go where he is in heaven, and he can't come where we are," I said. "But we can always remember him and love him."

I set the daddy candle, still burning, in a cup. And we played with the other candles a bit more, moving them together, moving them apart. I explained that I would always love David, even if I loved Jeff, too. "Even if I give some love to Jeff, I still have lots of love for David, too," I said, moving my candle from one to the other.

David was soon smiling and ready to run off and play. Jeff and I talked about how profoundly moving the candle experience had been for us. We wondered if it had helped David.

A few days later, David was pretending to talk to his father again on his toy phone. "Daddy, is it okay if I love Jeff?" he asked. He looked at me to provide the Daddy voice.

"Yes, David, that would be really nice if you could love Jeff and he could love you," a shaky Daddy voice said. "I'll always love you, but I can't be with you now on Earth. So I think it's nice if you and Mommy have other people to love and other people who love you."

David flashed me a grin. "Thanks, Daddy," he said, and gently hung up the phone.

Julie McMaine Evans

READER/CUSTOMER CARE SURVEY

We care about your opinions! Please take a moment to fill out our online Reader Survey at **http://survey.hcibooks.com.**
As a **"THANK YOU"** you will receive a **VALUABLE INSTANT COUPON** towards future book purchases
as well as a **SPECIAL GIFT** available only online! Or, you may mail this card back to us.

(PLEASE PRINT IN ALL CAPS)

First Name _____ MI. ___ Last Name _____

Address _____ Email _____ City _____

State _____ Zip _____

1. Gender
☐ Female   ☐ Male

2. Age
☐ 8 or younger
☐ 9-12   ☐ 13-16
☐ 17-20   ☐ 21-30
☐ 31+

3. Did you receive this book as a gift?
☐ Yes   ☐ No

4. Annual Household Income
☐ under $25,000
☐ $25,000 - $34,999
☐ $35,000 - $49,999
☐ $50,000 - $74,999
☐ over $75,000

5. What are the ages of the children living in your house?
☐ 0 - 14   ☐ 15+

6. Marital Status
☐ Single
☐ Married
☐ Divorced
☐ Widowed

7. How did you find out about the book?
(please choose one)
☐ Recommendation
☐ Store Display
☐ Online
☐ Catalog/Mailing
☐ Interview/Review

8. Where do you usually buy books?
(please choose one)
☐ Bookstore
☐ Online
☐ Book Club/Mail Order
☐ Price Club (Sam's Club, Costco's, etc.)
☐ Retail Store (Target, Wal-Mart, etc.)

9. What subject do you enjoy reading about the most?
(please choose one)
☐ Parenting/Family
☐ Relationships
☐ Recovery/Addictions
☐ Health/Nutrition
☐ Christianity
☐ Spirituality/Inspiration
☐ Business Self-help
☐ Women's Issues
☐ Sports

10. What attracts you most to a book?
(please choose one)
☐ Title
☐ Cover Design
☐ Author
☐ Content

TAPE IN MIDDLE; DO NOT STAPLE

BUSINESS REPLY MAIL
FIRST-CLASS MAIL PERMIT NO 45 DEERFIELD BEACH, FL

POSTAGE WILL BE PAID BY ADDRESSEE

Chicken Soup for the Father & Son Soul
3201 SW 15th Street
Deerfield Beach FL 33442-9875

FOLD HERE

Comments

Do you have your own Chicken Soup story
that you would like to send us?
Please submit at: **www.chickensoup.com**

3

WHEN WE WERE YOUNG

*To this day I can remember my father's voice,
singing over me in the stillness of the night.*

Carl G. Jung

Letters to a Teenager

The only thing we know for sure about future developments is that they will develop.

Anonymous

Monday
Son,
   Good morning, unless of course you slept past noon, again. While I am at work, please mow the lawn and put the grass clippings in the recycle bin (not under the house).
   Afterward, please walk your sister down to Lisa Rangale's home. If Mrs. Rangale speaks to you, please don't grunt. Try using some of that English language you learned at school. How's the job hunting going? Is it tough finding summer employment halfway through the summer?
Love,
Dad.

P.S. Did I adopt your friends and not know it? One of them asked me for $10 the other day, and another wanted to know when Grandma was visiting. Then there's the kid who's been on the couch for six weeks with the remote control in his hands. He's wearing my pajamas.

Tuesday
Son,
   Good afternoon. The guest bathroom is for guests. You are not a guest—even though you act like one. Were we invaded yesterday by a band of pirates? There's not a lick of food in the house—even the baking soda is gone. Guard the Jell-O with your life.
Love,
Dad.

P.S. Are those your initials you mowed into the lawn?

Wednesday
Son,
   Good afternoon. If you are going to kiss your girlfriend, please have the courtesy to do it inside, rather than in front of the mailboxes and blocking Mrs. McCurdy next door from getting her mail. She's seventy-two and was grossed out. You're not too old for summer camp, you know.
Love,
Dad.

P.S. I noticed you and your friends all bleached your hair yesterday. Whose idea was it to do the same to the cat? She's fixed and declawed—wasn't that enough for her to handle?

Thursday
Son,
   Good afternoon. Is that our toilet paper hanging in Mrs. McCurdy's trees? I recognized our light blue two-ply. I'm

not sure what music you were listening to in your room last night, but before you bite the head off a bat or something, I think we should talk. Any idea when you might finish mowing the lawn?
Love,
Dad.

P.S. I hope you have a nice day at home. I'm thinking about licensing our place as a youth hostel. Tell your friends I'll give them a special rate if they take their feet off the coffee table.

Friday
Son,

Good afternoon. The garage sale was an interesting and ingenious idea to compensate for your summer unemployment. However, I wish you had mowed the lawn before you sold my lawn mower. What's your position on military academies?
Love,
Dad.

P.S. Someone's mom called this morning looking for her son. I asked her to describe the boy, but she couldn't remember what he looked like anymore (wait till she sees the hair). Anyway, she's coming over tonight to watch you kids eat—she's looking for the one who chews with his mouth open (I hope he has some other distinguishing mark). I pray it's not your friend who helped me push my car to the gas station this morning after you boys ran it dry last night. He bought me a doughnut and called me sir. I'd miss him terribly.

Ken Swarner

Dad's Shadow

Jeremy wriggled with excitement as he struggled to don his heavy laser-tag vest. "We're gonna beat you, Mom!"

"What are you talking about? You can't even get your gear on." I smiled as I tousled his blond hair and helped him buckle a strap around his waist.

Jeremy picked up his gun and walked with his father to sit in the waiting area while his older brother, Brian, and I finished suiting up. "We're on the same team, right, Dad?"

Stan grinned down at his munchkin partner. "You bet, Buddy. You just stick with me."

A couple of minutes later, the Funplex employee walked in. "Looks like you folks are the only ones here for this round. Have you played before?"

We shook our heads.

"Okay, I need to give you a few instructions." After going through the routine, he turned us loose into an enormous, dark room with walls and barricades painted black. Smoke hung in the air, giving everything an eerie appearance. Colorful lights flashed randomly, and loud music echoed from the high ceiling.

Brian and I charged our guns and located the base we

needed to protect. The whole time, I wondered whether Jeremy would be afraid in this strange environment. I needn't have worried.

As soon as the game began, Stan and Jeremy charged us and opened fire. Jeremy glued himself to Stan's side and mimicked every move his dad made. Whenever Stan ran to another barricade, Jeremy ran with him. Whenever Stan shot at one of us, Jeremy shot, too. He became adept at hiding just behind Stan's left leg, making it impossible to target him. In the dark room with his black laser-tag vest, he looked like a small shadow, a miniature version of his dad. Before I knew it, the fifteen-minute game was over, and I had hardly gotten off a shot the entire time. Brian hadn't fared much better.

"We won!" Jeremy shouted as he and Stan high-fived each other.

After hanging up the equipment, we walked out front to get our scores. The computer had assigned each of us an identity.

"Hey, Jeremy, look what the computer called you," Brian said, picking up the cards. "Shadow."

Stan patted his young son on the shoulder. "You sure were my shadow in the game today, Buddy."

Jeremy smiled. "That's my nickname from now on. I'm Dad's Shadow."

True to his word, Jeremy remained close to his dad. Their shared fascination with technology offered frequent opportunities for them to work together. When Jeremy was nine, they assembled a computer. When he was twelve, they created a website for a local radio station. Whatever interested Dad, interested Jeremy. No matter what project Stan worked on, he could count on his Shadow being right by his side.

As is often the case during the teen years, however, Stan and Jeremy found themselves increasingly at odds.

Too alike in personality, they clashed over the simplest things. Tempers flared whenever they worked together, and they rarely finished a project without one of them leaving the room in anger. The conflicts cast a different kind of shadow over their relationship.

The shadow lingered as the college years approached. Despite his aptitude with computers, Jeremy determined he didn't want to be a computer programmer like his dad. Instead, he enrolled in graphic design. After one semester, he realized that field wasn't for him and switched to computer networking, where he settled in like a mouse on a mouse pad. Occasionally, he even asked his dad's advice about a homework assignment. As Jeremy neared completion of his networking degree, he decided maybe he did enjoy writing computer code after all and signed up for a second degree—in programming. The sun came out, and Stan could see his Shadow once again.

When Jeremy turned twenty-one, he bought a custom license plate for his Jeep. He didn't even have to think twice about what he wanted on it: SHADOW.

Tracy Crump

The End of the Pier

If you can dream it, you can do it.

Walt Disney

"Dad! You're famous!"

Philip, Aidan, and Brennen ran into my study, eyes wide and looking at me as if I were Superman.

"Your picture was in the newspaper? How old were you? What happened?"

We had been vacationing in Pensacola, Florida, when my dad, my best friend, and I decided to do some fishing in nearby Navarre. A monstrous pier went a half a mile or so into the Gulf of Mexico. Because we had only two fishing poles, my dad bought me an open-faced rod and reel combo so we would have enough to keep us busy. It was a beautiful Shimano: silver and black. I imagined myself a great sea captain pulling in record swordfish and tarpon. Dad gave us casting lessons the first day. No telling just how many cigar minnows we scattered in the water below between tangles, but after a few hours, we became proficient and were able to focus on the fishing instead of the throwing. We fished a little while and noticed the action occurring at the end of the pier.

The end of the pier was the place of arrival. It was the bastion of seasoned anglers. To make it to the end meant you were recognized unofficially by the pier community. You were a true fisherman; someone from Hemingway. The fishing was truly better there, so in reality, the guys who made it to the end might have only been average but appeared great because of their constant hits. To a kid of nine these guys were mythological; masters of the sea.

Nothing was more impressive than when the masters hooked a monster. At the first whine of the reel an audience would gather. I remember the first guy I saw fighting a king mackerel. He sat up on the corner rail daring the fish to pull him into the waves. His arms bulged and his legs wrapped tightly around the rail as he held his rod straight up in the air. The tip of his rod doubled, pointing down into the deep. As he pulled the rod to himself, he reeled in the slack. The wind whistled, blowing around the taught line. A crowd amassed to cheer and some dared to offer advice.

My dad leaned down and whispered, "Watch and learn."

Finally the old man conquered the sea, and the king lay dethroned, humbled on the pier. People clapped, they slapped one another's backs, and cameras clicked. I caught a glimpse of something that is found only in dreams: greatness.

If only I could catch a fish like that and make it to the end of the pier.

After two days we hooked a couple of bonito but lost them as our lines were tangled with other fishermen pressing for position. We fished in the hot Florida sun for hours, watching others pull in monsters while we held on to nothing but hope.

On the final day of fishing, my dad decided to let us try

some live bait. All we would have to do is cast it out, watch our poles, and let the baitfish do the work. I cast my bait and went over to grab a Coke. It was nice to have a break from the pressure. All I had to do was just watch my rod tip as it lightly bounced up and down from the swimming baitfish. One more big swig of Coke and I would relax—that was until I looked over my can and saw my rod heading up and over the rail like a one-manned seesaw! I grabbed the rod and lifted it high to the sky, and the reel opened with a solo. The notes were loud and long as the fish on the other end headed out to the deep. Now began the difficult trek of stepping over rods and ducking under lines to the coveted end of the pier.

Earlier that week when we had hooked some fish, we had tangled about half a dozen people who wanted to keep their position as these two "young kids" tried to land their first fish. This time, people were quite willing to help me get to the prime spot for fighting the fish.

And fight I did!

I labored, pulling and reeling in the slack, thinking that when I worked the fish in, I could gaff it and bring it up . . .

But not this fish!

As soon as I got him close, my rod sang again, and out to the deep he swam. After fifteen minutes of these rounds, the crowd gathered behind me. "What is it?" Someone asked, and others mumbled, "This is no ordinary fish."

The masses cheered me, saying things like, "Hang in there!" and, "You're doing great!" Finally after another round of bringing it in, a man yelled, "Shark!" My eyes bulged and I felt the blood leave my face. Just on the other end of my hook was the thing of my nightmares, the creature haunting me since the movie *Jaws*. The shark turned and headed back out to sea, and my nine-year-old arms felt like Jell-O. All I could hear was eerie John Williams' music, and I was ready to call it quits.

Exhausted and scared, I turned to my dad and asked if he would take the rod. "No way, son," was his response. "Never give up!" My muscles burned from the constant pulling, but letting go meant quitting and even losing the rod my dad had given me. I had to go on. The crowd cheered, resounding louder and louder while others coached me. Nobody on that pier wanted me to quit. After a half an hour, I finally had the shark close enough to see. It was a beautiful gray with brownish spots like a leopard and was as long as I was tall. I lost so many other fish at this point that I was waiting for this one to break my line as well.

But not this time.

The moment of truth came. Some men gaffed the shark and raised it onto the deck. Still fighting and snapping its jaws, he flung his body in his fight to the death. All the while standing over him was a scared nine-year-old from Tennessee who had not caught anything bigger than a "river cat."

After the cameras gave out, my dad rushed to find a taxidermist. He would be crazy not to hang it on our wall. After we came home, he wrote our local newspaper. His mission was for the world to hear about his son landing a man-eater, a real David and Goliath story. To our surprise the article was printed and the story was told year after year in our family.

That was twenty-six years ago. Seeing the faces of my boys oohing and aahing about my victory over Jaws, I once again felt the exuberance of the day and the greatness of the end of the pier. Nevertheless, the end of the pier paled in comparison to the greatness I felt when my boys marveled at their discovery of their dad.

Scott T. Gill

A Father's Christmas Eve Rescue

Most of the important things in the world have
been accomplished by people who have kept on
trying when there seemed to be no hope at all.

Dale Carnegie

One of my great joys as a father is the annual tradition of playing Santa Claus on Christmas Eve. After the Christmas story is read, after the hot cider is gone, and after the last child is finally tucked away in bed, my wife and I spend a couple of hours scurrying throughout the house, producing presents from closets, drawers, under beds, and from places far too secret to mention here, lest my children find out.

Having performed this pleasant ritual for several years now, I have encountered more than once the maddening discovery that a special gift to one of my children lacks a particular part or battery or other accessory, something absolutely necessary for its proper functioning on Christmas morning. Sometimes I am able to make a last-minute save so that the gift will be complete, just the way Santa would have presented it. But I don't know if I could perform the feat of heroism my father did one Christmas Eve when I was four years old.

That crisp Texas night, sometime after the Christmas story had been read, after the hot cider was gone, and after the last child was finally tucked away in bed, my father got out his tools, began to insert screw "A" into bolt "B" and proceeded to assemble a shiny new green pedal car. The present was to be my first pretricycle venture onto wheels. He knew I would be excited . . . no, more than excited. He knew I would be delirious when I climbed into the car, grabbed the steering wheel, and pedaled it across our small living room on Christmas morning. The assembly job proceeded well, until he discovered the dreaded "Father's Christmas Eve Nightmare." To his horror, one of the car's wheels was missing.

I am sure that most fathers, including myself, after mumbling rude things about the kiddy car manufacturer and the store that sold it to them, would spend a few minutes rehearsing an apology to tell their children on Christmas morning and then simply go to bed. The really creative ones might manufacture a "letter" from Santa promising a new wheel just as soon as he could ship it from his North Pole workshop. But few fathers would do what my dad did that Christmas Eve.

He must have been very frustrated or very caring. He was certainly very determined. Since he never drank a drop of alcohol, he was without a doubt very sober, too. But some time in the predawn hours of Christmas Day, he climbed into his Studebaker sedan and drove ten miles to Leonard Brothers department store in downtown Fort Worth, where he had bought the deficient vehicle. What he was thinking I cannot speculate, but I promise that what follows is absolutely true.

After parking on the street in front of the store, my father began to walk around the dark building, knocking on its plate glass windows and doors. After several minutes of this, and most likely risking arrest in the process, my father attracted the attention of a security guard. The guard opened a door and asked his weary visitor what he wanted. My father explained the problem. Perhaps because of my father's sincerity or his urgency, or perhaps because the guard had small children himself, the man did an amazing thing. He let my father come inside the store. Accompanying him to the toy department, the guard watched as my father rummaged around until he found a wheel that fit the pedal car. Triumphantly returning home, my father finished assembling the miniature roadster before his children awoke.

When I think about this, I am amazed. I'm amazed because in our modern world where cynicism and mistrust are counted as wisdom, in our day when crime knows no holiday, a security guard would never take the chance that one had, especially in a major city's downtown area. I'm amazed that my father went to such extremes. But one thing that amazes me even more than how times have changed or how determined my father was, is that my father never told me about this extraordinary incident. When he died nine years after this took place, he took his secret with him. My mother didn't tell me about it until more than twenty years after the fact. Most dads, and I include myself, wouldn't be able to resist bragging to their kids about how they "saved Christmas." But not him. He didn't need the praise; he didn't want the applause. And he had already earned the respect of his children in other ways. Apparently the only reward he sought and the only one he required was my blissful and ecstatic smile on Christmas morning when I found my new car under the tree, its green paint glimmering in the multicolored tree lights, with every single piece in place.

Nick Walker

Full House

Youth is wholly experimental.

Robert Louis Stevenson

Four boys certainly made a full house for Dad and Mom. Roy, twelve, was a Second Class Boy Scout, and Joe, ten, a Sea Scout. Bill, six, and I, eight, were too young to be troublesome yet. This was my father's logic in convincing Mom it was okay for the two of them to go out for the night.

With an admonition to leave the coal furnace alone, our folks went off for a rare evening in town. What happened next is not quite clear . . . after all, I was so young (too young to be troublesome?).

Did Joe actually push two wooden boxes into the furnace and leave the fire door open? Accounts vary depending on which of the four of us you ask. But we all agreed that when the basement caught fire it was spectacular. Joe called the fire department. He yelled, "This is Jody, our house is on fire!" And hung up. Was his reputation so widespread that the fire department knew where "Jody" lived, or did a neighbor call it in? Who knows? But the firemen did arrive. And four scraggly kids stood outside the house in awe—and maybe in the beginning of terror.

Firefighters, fire trucks, and even an ambulance rushed to the scene, and I believe the appearance of all the boy-friendly machines, the sirens, and the general uproar kept us more excited than scared. What little boy doesn't want a fireman talking to him, picking him up, making sure he's okay? Neighbors were on the scene, too, and I guess it was the first time I ever saw how really caring people were. One after another, the neighbors took us under their wings and into their homes while the firefighters did their job.

At midnight, Mom and Dad returned home to a dark house with a police officer standing in the doorway. "Your house has burned, Mr. Firman, and your boys have been farmed out to various neighbors." Wow!

Fast forward to the retribution—the four prescribed spankings. Roy, first in and first out, said to yell as loud as possible because Dad had a soft heart and lacked a heavy hand. Joe and I each set off a cacophony that ensured a minimal spanking. But Bill, the little rat, bawled so piteously that he never suffered a single swat.

I wonder sometimes what Dad's punishment was for trusting us. Did Mom let him off the hook as easily?

Despite the mildness of the punishment—considering the seriousness of our "crime"—Dad had taught his sons a lesson that, despite many further antics, we didn't forget. We never burned another of our houses. But then again, Dad never left us home alone again either!

Win Firman

"Sorry, Dad . . . It won't happen again."

Things I Learned from My Dad

Things I didn't learn from my dad:

I didn't learn to tie a fishing lure.

I didn't learn to zero in a rifle.

My dad didn't teach me to shoot a bow and arrow or which bait to use for catching bass.

However, I did learn these things from my dad:

I learned to throw a spiral, turn two on the outside of my glove, and how to shoot a jumper.

I learned that to play a sport requires dedication, work, and effort.

I learned that to go through the motions is not enough on or off the field.

I learned that to teach young players the intricacies of the game is truly a privilege and should be treated as such.

I learned that watching football is not a spectator sport.

I learned to coach with my arms crossed and my hand on my chin, just like my memories of my father coaching.

I learned that no matter how much my father loved to coach, he walked away from it to spend more time with us.

I learned that Brooks Robinson was the greatest third

baseman ever to play the game, and there will be no discussion otherwise.

I learned that few memories are more precious than sitting in the upper reserve seats of Memorial Stadium as a kid with Dad watching Doug DeCinces throw his glove up in the air to knock down fly balls, except maybe sitting on the first-base side of Camden Yards as a teenager watching Cal take the field, except perhaps as an adult watching a game on the third-base side of Iron Bird Stadium and ducking foul balls with Dad.

I didn't learn how to change the oil in my car; I didn't learn to rotate my own tires, and I didn't learn to bleed my car's brakes, replace a muffler, or what in the world a "Hemi" is.

I learned that whatever was at the office that cold winter day was less important than coming home early to get into a snowball fight with my brother and then take us sledding.

I learned that regardless of the type of activity or sporting event, my father and mother would be there.

I learned that few things are more fun than standing at the top of a black diamond trail named the Jaws of Death in southern Vermont in twenty-two-degree weather with my father and brother daring each other to see who goes first.

I learned that my father's moustache freezes if it gets cold enough on the lift ride.

I learned that a solid shot off the first tee box on a crisp late September day with my brother and father along for the round is the definition of Perfect Morning.

I learned that I am a Smith, and with that comes certain expectations; it is my job to live up to them.

I learned that family is always family, even if they get on your nerves.

I learned to respect my mother always because she is not just my mom, she is my father's wife.

From my father I did not learn to run a jigsaw, I did not learn to use a nail gun, I did not learn how to build a deck or put plumbing in.

I learned that horseshoes is a competitive sport, and when my dad, "Captain Clutch," is hot, it is better to sit back and watch a true master at work, but I won't sit down because I learned never to give up—ever.

I learned it is okay to walk away from a bad situation but never to let someone chase you away.

I learned that my father was once not only thrown out of a softball game, but also out of the tournament and facility and was escorted to the city line. I tell this only to illustrate that my father made a mistake and admits it.

So I then learned my father was human and was one to take responsibility for himself.

I learned that a father who can do a front handspring can be somewhat embarrassing, but also is pretty cool.

I learned that it is better to do a lot than to have a lot, because possessions fade but memories always remain.

I learned that if Edgemere were a city, my father would be mayor.

I learned that there isn't a team he won't coach, a committee he won't sit on, and a fund-raiser he won't support as long as it helps the kids.

I learned that to serve one's community is a great undertaking but to serve one's country is truly one of the greatest.

I learned that my dad is the greatest tour guide that ever walked the paths of Disney World.

Finally, I learned that friends and family are the greatest possessions a man can have and he can never have enough.

So in closing, my dad never taught me how to hang dry-wall; I never learned to hunt a deer or how to flush the radiator in my car.

But that's okay because I can take a class or read a book to learn that.

I learned how to be a friend, a man, a husband, and a father. I only learned that by having an example to watch and learn from, and I had one of the best.

Bob Smith

This Matchup Will Always
Rank as a Classic

It was an all-time classic matchup, ranking right up alongside Bill Russell versus Wilt Chamberlain, Arnold Palmer versus Jack Nicklaus, Tiger Woods versus a dogleg par 5. It was Babe Ruth versus a fastball, Jesse Owens versus the stopwatch. Indeed, Ali and Frazier had nothing on this rivalry. It was Bird against Magic and USC challenging UCLA and Sampras opposing Agassi rolled into one. More than that, it was David and Goliath: The Sequel. What we had here was the aging, wily master versus the young, cocksure upstart. Brain against brawn, experience against quickness. Veteran versus rookie. One-on-one. No pennant was at stake, no world championship title to be won. Spoils to the victor did not include fame and fortune, a Nike contract, or one's picture on a Wheaties box. Still, the two combatants—my pop and me—went at it tooth and nail.

Pride was on the line. In his heyday, the cagey veteran had been considered a BMOC—Big Man on Court. He not only remembers the days when six-foot-four college centers were in vogue—he actually was one at tiny

Wittenberg University in Ohio. The rookie, on the other hand, was the prototype playground junkie. A gym-rat guard quicker than e-mail, with more moves than a bachelor in a singles bar. (Which, by the way, was only fitting, since at the time I was a bachelor—as most preshavers tend to be.) He dribbled with the sleight of hand of a magician and could shoot more accurately than Robin Hood.

The rookie wore out nets faster than he did the knees of his Levis. When he should have been in his bedroom hitting the books, he was often outside on the driveway hitting jumpers. The vet was a master of the medical boards, but the rook was a master of the backboards. We're talking Dr. J (J as in Junior) versus Doc (as in M.D.). The vet had lost a step in recent years. Maybe two. Perhaps even three. In the late summer of his life, the spring in his legs had long since sprung. But with the dog days of summer barking long into the warm evening, his aging bones would be magically transformed and he would feel twenty years younger. Challenged, he was once more a BMOC. And yet the vet's labored hustle and labored breathing were no match for the upstart's tireless energy. Nor was his old-fashioned 1940s-era set shot half as deadly as the rookie's soft-arching "J." But in addition to guile and experience, the crafty old pro had one more asset on his side of the ledger: the Hook. An unstoppable weapon.

Don't be misled. The Hook was not of the famed "Skyhook" perfected by the NBA's all-time scoring king Kareem Abdul-Jabbar. No, it was not launched from out of the clouds or arena rafters. It didn't even come from out of the eucalyptus treetops lining the driveway court. Rather, it was a sweeping shot released with a stiff arm from about the ten o'clock position. What's more, it came ambidextrously, from both wings. Right-handed. Left-handed. Left-handed. Right-handed. It was like a windshield wiper gone berserk. Not a soft shot, the Hook banged the wooden backboard—*bam*—like a judge pounding his gavel, and rendered its own form of justice two points at a time. Make no mistake, the Hook was no "brick" that broke the backboard or bent the rim. The only thing the Hook broke was the opponent's morale. Its unique sidespin—"English" is the word the old pro used to describe it—literally made the basketball dive off the backboard and through the net, like a diver knifing cleanly into a deep blue pool. Shoot. *Thwack! Swish!* Two points, side out. To the dwarfed rookie, the Hook was as unstoppable as the common cold. The kid was like a sandcastle defending a rising tide. It was the great equalizer for Father Time.

Thus the showdown featured the Hook seasoned with a few one-hand set shots, versus twenty-foot jumpers and occasional drives. On and on the games went—winner's outs, first one to ten by ones—and then a rematch, and a re-rematch until darkness fell or dinner was called.

Four decades later it remains unknown who came out ahead in the long history of this torrid series. Each claims he did. Both know it doesn't really matter.

Similarly, a new series is underway, one where I have switched jerseys and am the cagey vet against my teenage rookie-son. With drug scandals and contract holdouts and labor strikes littering the sports pages, it's refreshing to see a sporting matchup played for the pride of it. For the fun of it. Where the sounds of skin-on-skin fouls are muffled not by arguments, but by echoes of laughter. Don't believe that sports are still fun and games to some? Check out any driveway that has a basketball hoop at the end of it—and watch the new classic one-on-one basketball matchups between fathers and sons (and daughters, too!).

Woody Woodburn

Building Your Dreams

A man can do only what he can do. But if he does that each day he can sleep at night and do it again the next day.

Albert Schweitzer

"Not another apartment!" I've heard that statement a few times. Working as an apartment manager for two years brought me in contact with various applicants and their opinions. Many of them were tired of living in crowded rentals with little privacy and walls so thin that neighbors heard their every move. They longed for a spacious backyard for their children to play in, a garden with vine-ripened tomatoes, and enough room for the family dog to bury his favorite bone. These renters all had one dream in common: owning their first homes.

However, to make these dreams come true, most people need the help of a loan institution. They must have established credit, money set aside for a down payment, and sufficient income to maintain payments for the next thirty years.

Not my father, Raymond; he dreamed up a different way to own a home.

Dad had bartered several tile jobs in exchange for a vacant lot nestled near the foothills of the San Gabriel Mountains in Southern California. The next month, he and my mother, Eloise, started construction on their first house, one piece at a time.

During the building process, my father worked as a fire-fighter for the Los Angeles County Fire Department. It was a good job with steady work. Still, his salary barely covered the bills. Money was tight in those days, just like today. Nevertheless, after each payday, he stopped by the La Canada lumberyard on his way home. With any extra cash from his paycheck, he purchased building materials.

Dad enjoyed challenges. He mixed his own cement and poured the foundation with the help of a borrowed wheel-barrow. The living room and bathroom were the first things to go up. My parents lived in the living room, cook-ing their meals over the open fireplace while they finished the kitchen. After the kitchen came their bedroom, and then they were finished.

After my sister, Nita, was born, they moved her into the living room. I realized later why my parents called it the "living" room: it was a place one lived in while waiting for a "real" room. The sleeping arrangements were viable until I came along three years later.

When I was born, my parents had a dilemma: where to put me. Since the living room was already at capacity, they placed me in a secondhand crib at the end of the hall-way, adjacent to the bathroom. For the next four years, the back of the hall became my five-foot dormitory. My par-ents called it the hall-room. I could visit the living room during the day, but I had to return to the hall-room for the night.

I have always favored the story of Cinderella because we had something in common—our own little corner in the house. However, unlike Cinderella's family, my family loved me very much. My cramped accommodations were the best my parents could offer. Needless to say, I didn't invite many friends for sleepovers. As I grew older, I envied my sister's spot in the living room.

One morning, I heard someone digging outside the house. When I rushed outside to see who was making all the noise, I discovered my father digging a long trench along the back of the house, adjacent to hall-room. Finding a broken shovel in the backyard, I offered to help, making sure to stay out of his way. I had no idea what he was doing, but it looked like fun. Besides, I liked playing in the dirt.

During the next few weeks, we dug a trench about twenty feet long on each side, forming a perfect square at the back of the house. We finished by digging a smaller ditch that ran down the middle, connecting both ends with each other. The next week, a delivery truck arrived with a load of sand, rock, and heavy bags of gray stuff. When combined with water, the mixture made the best mud pies. Dad called it concrete. We shoveled our creation into the forms we had built earlier and let it dry.

My father let me help with every part of the building process, all except the electrical. I even nailed down a few of the roofing tiles. Mom worried most about my being on the roof, but Dad always assured her I would be fine. I never slipped even once.

Although I have forgotten many things about my child-hood, I will never forget building my first real room. Dad and I had such fun together. Digging forms, pounding nails, painting walls—it had never seemed like work at all. These memories are as unmovable as the concrete we poured.

When I turned nineteen years old, I moved away from home. That year, a specialist diagnosed my father with cancer. Dad died three years later. I wept for months, the loss was overwhelming. Even today, thirty years later, the tears still flow. I often wonder if Dad knew his life might end prematurely. Maybe that's why he let me help with the construction when I was so young. If so, he left something precious behind, something better than any earthly inheritance. Dad left me a heritage of faith, memories that will never fade, and he taught me how to build my dreams, one prayer at a time.

Occasionally, I take a trip to La Canada, California. I drive up Ocean View and make a right turn on Daisy Lane. The old house looks the same. My small handprint remains stamped into the concrete foundation, along with the words: "dad and me."

Charles E. Harrel

One Saturday Morning

There is only one happiness in life, to love and be loved.

George Sand

Saturdays were workdays at our home, unless they fell on a holiday or other special occasion. There were few exceptions. By the time I was a teenager, I had developed a strong dislike for weekend workdays. My perception remained unchanged until one Saturday morning.

We had two types of jobs around the house: chores and projects. My father usually assigned the chore to me and picked the project for himself. I learned long ago that there was a big difference between the two. Projects were more technical and required a certain amount of expertise, while chores required little more than hard labor. Projects were exciting and fun, while chores were boring and dismal. Trimming our plum tree was a project; picking up the fallen branches was a chore. I could recognize a chore anywhere.

After breakfast, I received my assignment for that Saturday, hauling scraps of wood—obviously a chore. These wood slats were the remnants of a previous workday involving a tattered fence. Dad would build a new fence later to replace it, which of course would be classified as a project.

Today's chore seemed simple enough: remove the slats blocking the driveway and stack them on the woodpile in the backyard. My strategy was to throw the wood over the front hedge onto our lawn below and after lunch haul it to the woodshed for stacking. After I started on the wood slats, my father undertook the anticipated project of hanging a new screen for the front porch. The old screen had rusted out long ago and even the patches had holes that needed repairing.

Halfway into the pile of wood, I lost focus on my task. When the boredom kicked in, which often happened with chores, I turned my assignment into a game—tossing pieces of wood high into the air. While the slats landed in the yard below, I pretended to be a champion javelin thrower going for the winning toss. My final throw won the gold medal.

Meanwhile, my father worked diligently to finish his project. As he stepped back for a moment to admire his finished handiwork, a wood slat arched through the air, pierced the middle of the new screen, and landed at his feet. It dangled in a slow arc like a spear after hitting its mark. Dad's face transformed into a look of utter amazement. He couldn't believe the new screen had lasted only a few seconds before being destroyed. When I heard my name called in that familiar tone, I knew a problem had unfolded that probably involved me.

Rushing to the front room, I saw an incredible sight of impending doom. Mom held her right hand over her heart in shock. Dad had just taken the dreaded deep breath—he seemed to hold it forever—never a good sign. Then I saw it, a piece of wood waving side to side in the wind, forming a perfect bull's-eye in the center of the screen door.

I was in unprecedented trouble, and the silence in the room was unbearable. Hastily, I considered my options: make up an excuse, plead guilty, or beg for mercy. Expecting a major scolding or worse, I just stared at the floor and waited. Making eye contact too soon might not be in my best interest.

Out of the silence, I heard a snicker, then another. Soon the belly laughs began. I looked up to see my father in a fit of hysterical laughter. Mom just stood there smiling, relieved. Dad should have grounded me for weeks, but instead he smiled, wrapped his big arms around me and said, "Ah, forget about it; I can fix it." Dad was still grinning to himself as he cut in a patch for the newly destroyed screen.

That was our last workday for the summer. Enrolling in college and working full time gave me an exemption from chores for the next several years.

A month before I graduated, my father died. The doctors said he had cancer. I miss Dad so much: his grin, his strong arms, the look of mercy in his eyes. Sometimes the sorrow overwhelms me. Yet with the sadness also comes the joy, and the memories of that one Saturday morning when I discovered how much my father loved me.

Charles E. Harrel

www.martybucella.com

"You have it easy. When I was your age, I had to walk all the way across the room to change the channel."

Be a Doctor

The harder you work, the luckier you get.

Gary Player

We lived in Brooklyn, five blocks from Ebbett's Field, and I was a rabid Dodger fan. To paraphrase a future Dodger manager, when I cut myself, I bled Dodger blue. I could quote the statistics of all the players, including their batting averages, fielding percentage, and ERAs. I even knew how the prospects in the Dodger farm system were doing. My father wished that I knew as much about my schoolwork. During the season, I saw the end of most home games because they let the kids in free after the seventh inning. I even managed to sneak into a few games after the first inning when the ticket takers weren't looking. I saw other children scream in their fathers' ears as they watched the game. But I never went to a game with my father. When the Dodgers were on the road, I was out in the street, practicing my swing with a broomstick and a Spalding ball.

I was ten years old in 1947, two years after the end of the war, and I had high hopes for my Dodgers bringing their first world championship back to Brooklyn. I was devastated when they lost again to the hated Yankees. My father was unsympathetic. "Why do you spend all your time on this foolishness? You'd be better off studying hard and make something of yourself—be a doctor."

"I want to be a baseball player and play for the Dodgers," I said. The look of disappointment on my father's face became engrained in my memory. Why couldn't he understand my love for baseball?

Later, I learned that my father had immigrated to this country at the age of eighteen, leaving his parents behind in Russia. He couldn't speak English and he had no high school diploma. In seven years, going to school mostly at night and working during the day, he obtained a high school equivalency certificate, completed college, and received a master's degree in chemical engineering. That's why he had no tolerance for wasting hours in nonacademic pursuits. At the time, though, I didn't understand and was deeply hurt by his actions. I wished that I could share my passion for baseball with him.

When the 1948 season started, I continued badgering my father to take me to a baseball game. His response remained constant. "I don't have time for that foolishness." My reaction also remained constant: I pouted but didn't let that stop me from sneaking into games or honing my baseball skills with my trusty broom handle.

When my teacher handed me the next-to-last report card for the year, it didn't faze me. It was pretty much the same as all my previous ones. The report card was divided into two sides. On the academic side, I received outstanding for math, science, and geography, and satisfactory for history, art, and English. On the deportment side, I had a number of unsatisfactories, including one for conduct. In the comment section, the teacher wrote, "Runs with scissors, interrupts other children, chatters incessantly, particularly about baseball."

When I showed the report card to my father, his disapproval bore into me again. I expected him to yell. Instead, he said, "I'll tell you what I'll do, young man. On your next report card, if you get all outstandings in the academic subjects and at least satisfactory in the deportment categories, I'll take you to a baseball game."

"I will, Pop. I will."

I sneaked into fewer games and put my broom handle into the closet. I memorized dates, times, places, and vocabulary words. I tried to keep my mouth shut in class, which was difficult for me. When the teacher handed out the next report cards, I held my breath. My hands trembled as I looked at mine. I had done it—all outstanding grades in academics and satisfactory in all aspects of deportment. The teacher wrote in the comment section, "Much improved!"

I glowed as I handed my father the report card. He did, too. "You pick out the game and I'll buy the tickets," he said.

I think I picked out a Saturday afternoon game with the Dodger's crosstown rivals, the New York Giants. I dragged my father there early on the day of the game so that we could watch batting practice. He bought me popcorn and a Coke. I had already come fortified with a box of Good 'n' Plenty and a Baby Ruth bar. I hoped that I'd be able to get my father to show an interest in baseball.

We had great seats along the first-base line. I had never been so close to the players. I saw Jackie Robinson, the first African-American player in the Major Leagues, and was excited because he had been the most valuable rookie the year before. The game started and the Giants quickly jumped into the lead. My father yawned.

"Don't worry, Pop. The Dodgers will come back."

By the fifth inning, the rout was on, and my father was

fast asleep. Thank goodness there was enough noise to drown out his snoring. After the seventh inning stretch, only dyed-in-the-wool fans like myself remained. I guess I had mixed feelings about my father still being asleep. On the one hand, I'd get to see the whole game. He wouldn't push to leave early. On the other hand, we weren't screaming together. I wasn't sharing my love for baseball. The game was about as interesting for him as watching test patterns on our new television set.

The Dodgers batted in the ninth inning trailing 11-2. My father continued to doze. The first batter singled up the middle, but was erased by a double play. The remaining fans edged toward the exits. Then the floodgates opened and the Dodger bats came to life. Hit followed hit. Soon the score was 11-6 and the Dodgers had the bases loaded. The crowd shrieked, which woke my father up. "What's happening?" he asked.

"I told you they'd come back."

Another single, then a walk, brought the score to 11-8, and the bases were still loaded. I got up on my chair and screamed. My father stood. Another single and the score was 11-10. I howled, and to my surprise, my father said, "This is terrific."

The next batter hit a grounder to short. *It's all over now,* I thought, but the shortstop booted the ball, loading the bases. I grabbed my father's sleeve. "We got lucky, Pop."

"We sure did." Then he screamed at the next batter, "Get a hit, you bum."

The next hitter smashed a screeching line drive down the third-base line. It looked like the Dodgers were about to win the game, when the Giant third baseman, who was guarding the line, made a leaping catch. I felt my heart sink. The Dodgers rally had fallen short.

I turned to my father and saw the look of disappointment on his face, the same look I was used to seeing when

I told him that I wanted to be a baseball player not a doctor. I must have had the same look, too. He put his arm around my shoulders and hugged me. With his thumb he wiped a tear from my eye. "I love you," he said.

I reached up and gave him a bear hug. "I love you, too, Pop."

We walked out of the game holding hands, and I waved the Dodger pennant he had bought for me. He gently squeezed and I squeezed back.

Paul Winick, M.D.

My Dad Was a Comic Book Hero

I stopped believing in Santa Claus when I was about ten.

I lost my faith in the Easter Bunny and the Tooth Fairy around the same time.

But I never stopped believing in Superman. How could I? He lived in my house.

The Superman under my roof didn't wear a red cape and boots. On most days I'd spy him in a white shirt and a tie, carrying a briefcase out the door before anyone else in the house was even out of their slippers.

I always suspected he was Superman because he fit the description so well. He was the fastest person I knew. I raced him on countless occasions and never came close to catching him except for the times he let me win.

As for strength, he was liable to swoop me up off the ground at any time and lift me high enough so that my back touched the ceiling.

And I knew he had some kind of X-ray vision because he always knew when I was telling the truth—and when I wasn't.

He could fix any break, kill any spider, and win any game. He possessed enough smarts to teach me math and enough patience to teach me how to hit a baseball.

And within the thick brown leather belt he wore on most days, he held the power of motivation. I can count on one hand the number of times he used it for anything besides securing his pants. But I never, ever forgot it was there.

He also held the power to take away my Big Wheel, my bike, and later, my car keys.

As I began making friends, I discovered a secret. They lived with Superman, too. All of my friends swore they did.

My dad owns a grocery store.

My dad's a heart surgeon.

My dad played football in college.

The boasts were big and they were sincere. Superman lived in everyone's house, apparently. Secretly, though, I knew the real Superman lived in mine.

I didn't hold that conviction forever, of course. Neither did my friends. By the time we were adolescents, the hero of our stories had become us.

Nothing maudlin here. Dads can't be Superman forever. Children grow up and parents grow old. It has always been that way. It's supposed to be that way.

But we suspend those rules on special occasions, don't we?

I used to rail against Father's Day for being artificial; it was probably the brainchild of some greeting card company marketing executive, right?

But Father's Day isn't really about the cards. It's about putting the red cape back on Dad's shoulders.

My dad is in his mid-sixties now, and most of the Superman claims I used to make about him have ceased to be true.

He's not the fastest guy on the block anymore; if we were to race again, I'd probably win nine out of ten. Okay, maybe six out of ten.

He's still strong, but not strong enough to lift me to the ceiling. That's a treat now reserved for his grandkids—the smallest of them, anyway.

He's not Superman in the way the comic books describe Superman. From the vantage of age and experience, I understand that he never was.

But the point is I believed he was once. He knew it, too. So did your dad. Most dads do—they accept that responsibility.

They try to live up to the impossible standard of Superman.

Forget the kryptonite of fatigue and financial responsibility. Forget the demanding boss and the need to hang out with the guys.

The best dads give it all up to play Superman as long as their children are willing to believe. Longer, actually.

Eventually, they all hang up their capes, but a special strength is to be found in that surrender as well.

A father myself, I'm now the one trying to impersonate Superman. Like most dads, I fall on this side of Clark Kent most of the time.

But retired supermen make great advocates for weary fathers. "No dad is perfect," they will tell you. "But children are able and eager to find the superhero behind the mask."

Powerful encouragement is in that advice. It's more powerful than a locomotive.

I guess that's a superpower dads keep for life.

Bob Dickson

4

THROUGH WOMEN'S EYES

The most important thing a father can do for his children is to love their mother.

Henry Ward Beecher

Lessons from the Dugout

Start by doing what's necessary; then do what's possible; and suddenly you are doing the impossible.

St. Francis of Assisi

You stood at the tee, staring out to the field, which seemed to reduce you to a small speck against a canvas of green grass and red dusty baseball dirt. Part boy and part baby, your knobby knees touched, and your rounded tummy pushed against the T-shirt hanging so low it covered your shorts. You raised the bat to your shoulder, just the way Dad had taught you. The large red batter's helmet wobbled on your head. From the splintered stands, behind home plate, I clutched my hands together. Dad was perfectly relaxed.

The coaches initially suggested we put you back in a younger league, with the four- to five-year-olds. "He's small for his age," they said. "He might get hurt." But I knew what they meant: Your son can't catch a ball. He doesn't run fast. And sometimes he misses when he swings. Dad spent hours in the front yard working with

you. Then he convinced the coaches to let you play with
the other six-year-olds. "Sending him back," Dad said,
"will break his spirit."

Thinking back on it now as we sat behind you, separated by a metal fence at your very first game, I wondered
if Dad and I had made a mistake. "The boy is so small." A
lump rose in my throat.

Dad patted my hand and said softly, "He'll be fine."

You took a practice swing. The other players and the
spectators quieted to a few scattered whispers. All eyes
were on you. My child. You drew the bat to your shoulder
again, ready for the real thing. *Please just let him get on first,*
I thought. *It will mean the world to him.* You swung the bat.
The motion was awkward and the bat was too high. You
missed the ball. I lowered my head to hide the sudden
rush of tears in my eyes.

Someone from the other team laughed. The coach patted you on the back and whispered in your ear. Then he
stood back, and you pulled up the bat again. With a timid
shift of your hips, you put all your forty pounds behind
the next swing. The ball flew from the tee and landed right
at the pitcher's feet. "He'll never make it to first," someone
said.

I'm not a screamer. I'm hardly competitive, and I don't
care for sports. But right then, as your feet left home plate,
I stood on my seat and yelled as loud as I could, "Run,
Ford! Don't look back, just run!" Dad yelled, too!

But the ball beat you to the base. You were out and the
inning was over. You ran with the other kids to the
dugout. I rushed to meet you, but you disappeared behind
the cinder-block wall. *Will the kids tease him?* I wondered.
Will he cry?

Dad told me to let it go. "It's all part of the game, part of
being a boy," he said. Dad knows that being part of a team
means learning to roll with the punches and that some-

times, oddly, males bond over ridicule and gentle teasing. "Do not go in the dugout," Dad told me.

For ten painful minutes you were invisible to me. I would never know what went on in the dugout. It wasn't my place. You had to learn this lesson on your own. Sometimes, I guess, being a parent means allowing you to have experiences that will break my heart while they build your character. But Dad's heart wasn't breaking. "He'll be fine," he said over and over to me.

You were at bat one last time for the sixth inning. We were separated by more than a metal fence now. In the dugout you had grown in ways I will never understand. But Dad does.

You planted your feet firmly in the dirt and pulled up the bat. The coach gave you an encouraging smile. You swung, but I couldn't bear to watch. Then someone yelled, "Run, Ford!" so I opened my eyes and saw you running to first. You made it! The crowd laughed as you did a victory dance. I laughed. Dad laughed, too. Two batters later, you were safe again on third. You looked to see if we were watching. The next batter hit the ball and you ran home. Then you circled back to the dugout, leaving us there, behind the fence at home base, where we will always be cheering for you.

Sarah Smiley

One of the Guys . . . at Last

"Good hit!"

My husband's voice floated back to me from the back-yard through our kitchen window. In it I heard grandfa-therly pride mingled with delight. Isaiah had just shown his eight-year-old baseball prowess and Granddad was duly impressed.

Not a big deal. Kids love to hit baseballs, and grandpas love to be on the pitching end. But the vignette lingered with me the whole day.

Having grandsons has enriched my husband's life in unexpected ways. This was a man who yearned to have sons but ended up with three complicated, fiery daugh-ters instead. He never once expressed disappointment when first Jill, then Amy, followed by Nancy came along in fairly rapid succession.

But I did catch a glimpse of his face moments after the doctor had told him the news—a third girl—just outside the delivery room (back in the ancient days when dads weren't present at births). I saw a look of surrender.

We would have no more babies. So, no little boys to monitor on the journey to manhood—just these little girls. And, alas, they didn't like baseball or many other sports.

My husband never admitted it, not even now, but I know he has always seen his basic role as protector of his daughters. No women's movement could change his rock-solid belief.

Our daughters grew up knowing that their father was their anchor, their silver-haired knight, who wore his heart on his sleeve. For better or worse, he was the man who would chase away the demons of their bad dreams when they were small, soothe their adolescent angst, and walk them down the aisle, or in our case, the garden path of our home, as each married in succession.

On the day our first grandchild—another girl—was born, I tried to read my husband's face. Was this yet another disappointment? Had he secretly yearned for a Jonathan, the name he was always going to give a son?

But his delight in this perfect miniature, a carbon copy of her mother, was so wide and deep that it seemed impossible to top.

A year later, our "baby" had a baby of her own. Nancy's news seemed almost unfathomable when we got the call on that November morning. Nancy had given birth to . . . Sam! And a brave new world had dawned on our family.

Today, we have not just three granddaughters, but also four grandsons, two of whom have an uncanny resemblance to their maternal grandfather. And now, toy trucks zoom around our family room, and little boys, all under the age of ten, seem to bounce off walls in their play. Their grandfather dries their tears when they fall or fight with one another, or when they feel sad or scared. He's a veteran of all of that.

He walks with each of them to a little pond near our house to watch the ripples pebbles make when they hit water. It's something he often did with their mothers.

But these days, he also has some new equipment in the garage: baseballs and gloves, Frisbees, a miniature football, and some "guy stuff," as he calls this accumulation of tools and toys he's been collecting. He can be found watching a football game with little boys who seem genetically pre-destined to share his excitement. Their mothers would sooner go shopping.

So I smile to myself and say nothing. But what a joy it is for me to see the man with whom I've shared my life opening this new chapter, this "man-to-man" chapter he is writing with little guys named Sam, Isaiah, Jonah, Daniel.

Someday our grandsons may understand how long and eagerly their grandpa has waited just to say the simple words, "Good catch!"

For now, I'm so grateful that at last, he's one of the guys.

Sally Friedman

The Photograph

There is no remedy for love but to love more.

Henry David Thoreau

It is one of my most treasured photographs—my husband and our then two-year-old son. My men were on the deck of a beach house enjoying a beautiful summer's day, gazing off in the same direction. Both were smiling in profile when I clicked the shutter and saved this joyous moment forever.

When my son was an art major at the University of Central Florida, he took this photo out of the family album and made a beautiful pencil drawing of their moment together. He then framed it and gave to my husband, who immediately hung our son's work of art on the wall of his office. Obviously, this picture had special meaning to us all.

Aside from the fact that my snapshot shows a good time (of which there are many), this photo is symbolic of the father-son relationship that exists in our family. Even twenty-five years after the picture was taken, both of my men are smiling and heading in the same direction. I suppose it all started when the doctor held up our newly born infant and it was abundantly clear that we had a son. The smile on my husband's face could have generated enough power to run all the delivery room electrical equipment. Not only was our family complete with a daughter and a son who could carry on the family name, but it was more than that. Now my husband had someone with whom he could share all of his masculine activities.

I remember my son as a toddler, following his father and carrying hammers and screwdrivers as we added a bedroom addition to our home. When my son was a little bigger, my men were often together under the sink fixing the latest plumbing crisis, or they were up to their elbows in sudsy buckets as they washed the cars together each Saturday afternoon. When my son was about four, my husband converted the backyard into an Ewok village in honor of my son's favorite movie, *The Return of the Jedi*. As I watched the two of them crawling through the bushes having some sort of Luke Skywalker adventure, I knew my men shared a very special relationship.

It was about that time in our lives that tragedy struck in our neighborhood. The mother of one of my son's school buddies died at the age of thirty-four of malignant melanoma. Our family tried as best we could to help her two boys and husband—babysitting, comforting, and just being there—but ultimately, family members had to endure the pain of loss we could only imagine. As time moved forward, their sorrow eased, and the father met, fell in love with, and married a new mother for his sons. Eventually their lives seemed to regain a normal rhythm.

As these events unfolded, my son must have been carefully watching and pondering the effects on his friend and his family. To me, my son appeared to be his usual cheerful self, but I didn't realize until sometime later that deep inside he had been empathizing with his friend. One night as I sat on the sofa reading, my son snuggled up to me and put his head on my shoulder.

"Mommy," he began, "do you think you will ever have to get me a new daddy?"

"Oh, I hope not," I replied, sensing his distress for the first time. "Why are you asking?"

"Well, I just wanted you to know that if you do ever get me a new daddy, I will always like this daddy best."

I don't remember what I said in reply. I probably didn't say anything, because I understood exactly what he meant and felt. I am sure I simply hugged my little man and thanked God for allowing him to know such a meaningful and loving relationship with his father, one that even death could not alter. Maybe that is why my beach day photograph holds such a dear place in my heart. My photo had clearly captured the rare bond between my son and his father, years before we even realized it for sure ourselves. As a result, it remains our favorite image.

Dorothy K. Fletcher

Strong Arm Needed

Our son, Erick, had a ball glove even before he was born. At six months, his dad was rolling a ball to him; at a year, he was tossing it to him. As Erick grew up, I would look in the backyard and see father and son throwing a baseball, a football, or a Frisbee. Inside they would tone it down and toss a Nerf ball, respecting my request.

For a time, Rick coached Erick's ball teams, and we lived through the tensions between coach-dad and player-son. *Why is Rick often harder on our son than on other boys? Why does he expect so much out of him? I hope this won't have a negative effect on their relationship.* Rick worked with Erick to help him develop basic sports skills. They still maintained an upbeat relationship after all the practices and games, for which I was thankful.

When Erick was older, Rick stepped back to allow others to coach him. Although he was careful to stay out of the way, I could tell that in his heart he wished he was Erick's coach.

Erick particularly loved football, although he was better at other sports. As a high school freshman he was small. We encouraged him to run cross-country, since he had the build of a natural runner. His friends wanted him to play football. So, to frustrate everyone, he chose to do nothing. Ugh! I thought the season would never end! He bugged me after school instead of being with the other boys at practice.

By his sophomore year, he had grown some and wanted to give football a try. *Okay, give it a try. It'll be only one year.* Just as Erick was beginning to improve, he broke his arm and was sidelined for the rest of the season. I knew this would happen! I wanted to say, "I told you so!" I wondered if maybe now he would get this football thing out of his system and he wouldn't go out again. On the positive side, the disappointment led to some great opportunities for father-son talks on dealing with setbacks.

The junior year came, and Erick had an intense determination to make up for lost time in developing football skills. *What? Another year of football? Do you want to get hurt even worse?* I resigned myself to the idea, and watched with curiosity and some fear as the season began. *Will he have the same determination demonstrated by his father's work ethic? Or will he be all talk and no action, like so many other teenage boys?*

Early in the season, Erick came home from practice tired, hungry, and looking for his dad. Rick had also just come home and was tired, hungry, and wanting to unwind.

"Dad, would you throw some passes to me in the backyard?"

Rick looked over to me as if to ask for permission to stay in if supper was ready. Instead, I nodded and gave the go-ahead.

He took a deep breath and sighed. "Sure, son. We've got time before supper."

They headed out to the backyard, where the crisp autumn air invigorated them both. I'm sure Rick thought that after a few passes he could come in and eat.

Time passed; it was getting dark, and supper was getting cold. Where were the guys? I looked out back, heard Rick shout, "Go deep!" and saw the football fly past.

Finally, I heard the backdoor open. Their father-son banter entered the house along with my two men.

Rick's shirt was darkened from perspiration, his face was red, and he was lamenting his sore arm. Erick had sweat on his brow and panted for breath, but was all smiles.

"Didn't think you could throw that many, Dad," Erick ribbed his father.

"Are you kidding? This arm is a rocket! I can keep up with you!"

He rolled his eyes at me.

This time I sighed. *Sure you can . . . just keep telling yourself that and maybe you'll believe it!*

Supper was now the priority for my ravenous men.

Putting food on the table, I asked Erick, "How'd it go?"

"Good."

End of conversation. The only sounds heard were forks hitting plates, and then Erick was off to complete his homework.

Over the next two months, this became the routine. Every night after football practice Erick asked his dad to throw to him until he caught 100 passes. And every night, Rick complied. Rick was committed to helping his son, and would not turn down Erick's request, no matter how tired he was. Erick was determined to be the best wide receiver he could be.

Erick gained confidence and steadily improved. He became a scoring threat to the opponents, and the opposing coaches planned double coverage on him.

Not only did Erick's skills improve, these backyard passing drills helped the father-son relationship grow. Erick pushed himself; Rick encouraged and supported him. Erick knew his dad was there for him no matter how he performed. Rick grew in knowing when to push Erick and when to back off.

As the mom, I cherished the fact that the son had picked up his father's work ethic and determination to be his best.

During his senior year, the football coach said that Erick actually willed himself to be a football player through determination and hard work.

That year his team won the state football championship.

We cheered and clapped during the awards presentation after the victory.

How proud I felt to see Erick standing tall on the field; he had proved me wrong about his participation in football. I smiled as I realized their father-son relationship had grown through the backyard passing drills. I glanced over at Rick and wondered if he was thinking the same. He was beaming—and rubbing his arm a little bit.

Nancy Kay Grace

"Of course I realize the importance of interactive play.
Tommy, change the channel."

The New Math

*One hundred years from now it will not matter
what kind of car I drove, what kind of house I
lived in, how much money was in my bank
account. . . . But the world may be a little better
because I was important in the life of a child.*

Forest Witcraft

I have a perfectly good calculator that calculates up to
twelve digits . . . even Donald Trump wouldn't require
more than that to count his billions. But when I sat down
recently and reflected on the staggering numbers my husband has logged while rearing his two sons over the years,
I quickly discovered that the calculator wasn't nearly
powerful enough.

At various ages and stages, a devoted father racks up
the big numbers! I was quite surprised to learn how that
looked for my husband over the course of his sons' lives:

- Logged 1,248 trips to the playground
- Chauffeured the boys to and from school on 4,836
  occasions

- Taught strategy for 1,872 hours as the kids learned their colors in Candy Land and the art of wheeling and dealing in Monopoly
- Pitched and caught balls for more than 2,081 hours (Of course, this does not include the time spent climbing over neighbors' fences and rocks to retrieve the myriad tennis balls that inevitably ended up in their yards!)
- Attended 468 hours of school conferences and recitals and cheered every accomplishment, big or small
- Supervised 2,418 hours of homework and assisted with those oh-so-special school projects that were "easy" for the kids to do on their own (I'm not sure our sons can build a volcano or replicate a living cell, but my husband now can!)
- Coached the Warrior soccer team and the Apache baseball team for a combined 1,466 sweaty hours
- Held his breath for 2,129 miles while giving driving lessons
- Lost 1,036 hours of sleep waiting up to be sure his teenagers arrived home safely
- Climbed 2,832 steps . . . and counting . . . while visiting prospective college campuses

Of course, this doesn't cover the countless hours he spent teaching the boys how to shave, tie a tie, tip the barber, or build that lightning-fast wooden car for the Cub Scout Pinewood Derby. It also doesn't include the countless hours he provided a strong role model of what a good husband should be . . . a lesson that is sure to pay dividends when the boys become husbands and fathers themselves.

So while Donald Trump may be considered a billionaire, the return on his investments doesn't hold a candle to my husband's. As his sons would surely agree, the return on their dad's investment of time in their lives is incalculable.

Pamela Hackett Hobson

The Fan Club

When my husband, Paul, was little, he was so skinny his mother fed him pure cream to try to fatten him up. He was a tow-headed runt and skinny as a rail. It didn't seem to matter how much he ate. Paul was wiry and a bundle of energy. His sisters tell me tales of how his mom tied pillows on his arms and legs when he learned to roller skate. She was so afraid he'd break something.

Needless to say, when our son Patrick was born, I wasn't surprised when he weighed in at six pounds and was only eighteen inches long. He was a tow-headed runt, too. But he was a healthy child, just like his father, and had his boundless energy embedded in his own genes.

When he played Little League, the first baseman would yell, "Easy out. This kid's a shrimp."

"He's little, but he's fast!" my husband would yell back.

Patrick would smack the ball, and in a whirl of dust he would run for first.

"Told you so!" my husband would yell proudly as Patrick took the base, much to the bewilderment of the other team.

About this time, I started working full time, and on

Saturdays I was extremely busy. I had the usual chores of laundry, grocery shopping, and running to the dry cleaners, not to mention chauffeuring Patrick's two sisters to dance class or gymnastics. I have to admit it wasn't my cup of tea to warm the bleachers every weekend, so I had an out. But Paul made all the Little League games; Patrick's faithful cheering team of one.

In high school Patrick joined the band; he played the cymbals. It wasn't long before he became a drummer and then head of the drum line. The band participated in many competitions every weekend, sometimes traveling as far as 100 miles on a bus just to bring home a trophy.

The band also made guest performances: Rose Parade, Rams games, Chargers games, Hollywood Lane Parade, and the Angels season-opening games. The booster club of parents traveled right along with them, and, yup, there was Paul cheering them on.

When the band wasn't competing, the drum line entered its own competitions. Every weekend was taken up by one competition or another. Paul was the consummate cheerleader, beaming with pride as his only son won again and again.

High school ended and so did Paul's weekend cheering when Patrick moved on to college. A few years went by, but Patrick and Paul stayed close, talking on the phone and both of them enjoying Patrick's weekend visits.

Then one Monday morning, Paul needed his own cheering section. He was undergoing a five-way heart bypass. The operation went smoothly, but I knew I might have problems with Patrick as we gathered in the recovery room. I was afraid he might crumble to see his hero lying so still and unconscious.

The *whoosh, whoosh* of the ventilator and the smell of the antiseptic filled the air as the family all trooped into Paul's room. I saw Patrick start to turn and leave. I knew he was having a hard time reconciling the sight of his pale, seemingly lifeless father with the strong man who was usually yelling encouragement from the stands.

Fighting back my own tears, I reached for his shoulder.

"Patrick, I know this isn't easy, but please do it for your dad. He was always there for you. This time be there for him."

Patrick looked at me through his tears and nodded. He went up and gingerly stroked his father's hand, the only part of his body where there was bare skin.

"I know you can't hear me, but I'm here, Dad. You're going to be fine. I love you and I need you. I'm your biggest fan."

Sallie Rodman

Three Peas in a Pod

On a beautiful summer afternoon, I sat under the tall redwood trees on a rustic log bench, watching my husband, James, and his father, Carl, throw horseshoes. The game of horseshoes takes practice and a certain amount of skill to perfect. Though I never played, my husband had explained and even demonstrated the different techniques involved in simply holding the horseshoe . . . then, of course, a player must stand a certain way to step off for the toss. Tossing the horseshoes can be done several ways, but James and Carl preferred holding the horseshoe on its side and making it flip a couple of times before reaching the peg. The game of horseshoes is a family tradition on my husband's side, and anytime we have a family gathering, you will find the men in the backyard tossing horseshoes. I should mention that most of the women could take on the men and hold their own as well.

This particular day it was just the two of them playing. I had brought Bradley, my four-year-old son, out to play on the tire swing, but he soon wearied of that and wanted to join his dad and grandpa at horseshoes. Grandpa handed him one, then bent down on one knee to show him how to hold it and how to swing his arm. James showed him how to step off and toss. Before long little Bradley had the hang of it. The three of them stood at the same end taking turns throwing their horseshoes. When all three had thrown, they walked side by side to the other peg and retrieved their horseshoes, counting points as they did. Bradley watched everything his dad and grandpa did and mimicked them closely. I was proud of how quickly he learned to play.

My mind wandered as the game continued, and I took a minute to give God thanks for blessing me with such a wonderful family. How blessed we were to be able to grow as a family and to have parents who taught our children such wonderful things as horseshoes!

I heard cheering and congratulations coming from the three players as my mind returned to the present. Bradley had gotten a "ringer"! Of course he was allowed to stand closer to the peg because of his age. My little guy beamed with pride and joy as he ate up the praise from his two heroes. As the three of them turned their backs to me and walked side by side to retrieve their horseshoes, I marveled at the similarity in them. All three walked with their shoulders held back, arms down at their sides; even their strides were the same . . . like three peas in a pod! I laughed aloud with the sheer joy of seeing something so touching, and I knew it was a memory I would never forget.

When my son was thirteen, we moved from California to my home state of Texas. There, our son and two daughters met their life mates, married, and started their own families. Many times I wish we were still living near my in-laws so that my grandchildren could grow up around their great-grand-parents. How wonderful it would be to see my grandchildren benefit from the values learned from their great-grand-parents' generation. Sadly, because of their advanced age and the miles between us all, I knew it would never be.

Recently James and I spent the weekend with our three children and thirteen grandchildren at the lake. We brought along a baseball and mitts, Frisbees, dominoes, board games, and, of course, horseshoes. I sat and watched all the activity around me. Two of my teenage grandsons were playing catch. My sons-in-law were playing dominoes, and my husband, son, and nine-year-old grandson were playing horseshoes. From the corner of my eye I just happened to catch the three of them walking back to retrieve their horseshoes. My eyes became misty and a lump formed in my throat. I laughed out loud with joy as I noted the three players walking with their shoulders held back, arms down at their sides, and even their identical strides . . . like three peas in a pod! I recalled a day years earlier as I marveled at history repeating itself. That's the moment I realized I didn't need to be sad at the absence of the great-grandparents in my grandchildren's lives. It was so obvious that they were present in every act, no matter how small, handed down from them to their son, James, and his son, Bradley, and his son, Nathan.

I stood and watched each activity around me and I saw myself in my daughters as they laughed, served plates, chased their little ones. I saw my mother-in-law and her mother when I heard my daughter say, "Well, I declare!" I saw my own mother in the way my children scolded their little ones, then loved on them to remind them they were loved. If I looked closely enough I could see mannerisms, speech, and actions reminding me of many loved ones now departed. As I watched my large family interacting, I wrapped my arms around my body, closed my eyes, and thanked God for reminding me of all life's blessings.

Christine M. Smith

Picture Perfect

Ed first met my husband, Paul, that fateful fall evening when he came to take my daughter to the junior prom.

"We don't have time for pictures," were the first words out of Ed's mouth as I pulled out my camera complete with a new roll of thirty-six exposure film.

"I think we do," Paul replied, standing his ground. And with that, the handsome young man in the black tux took his place in front of the drapes. Ed stood proudly next to my sixteen-year-old daughter, Jen. They looked at each other with sparkling eyes. Paul hoped this was a passing phase.

Later Paul asked me, "What type of guy meets the parents stating, 'We aren't doing pictures'? This definitely isn't the right guy for our daughter."

"Now, honey, give him a chance. You just met," I counseled, sure that it would be just another crush.

Evidently, Jen saw Ed differently, because they dated throughout high school and married a year later.

Paul tried to avoid butting heads with Ed, he really did. But they were both in love with the same woman, in different ways, but, oh, so competitive. And Ed was very headstrong. It wasn't that he was mean or cruel; he was just plain ole stubborn. They both were.

"Are Jen and Ed coming for dinner Sunday?" Paul would ask.

"Not this Sunday. Ed wants to take her to a new restaurant," I'd reply.

"Jen and Ed going to the movies with us next Saturday?" Paul would ask.

"Can't. They want to stay home alone by the fire."

And so it went.

Eventually, they moved an hour away from us to San Diego where his Navy base was located. My husband moped. His oldest daughter had been stolen right out from under his nose. At least, he saw it that way.

The happy couple bought a fixer-upper in San Diego. Paul arrived with his toolbox in hand, anxious to help fix up the place.

"Here to put that new fan in for ya," he said.

"Oh, no need, I'm doing it tomorrow," Ed replied.

"I'll fix that leaky faucet," Paul offered.

"Nah, I'm doing that next week on my day off," Ed said. On and on. Two stubborn males jockeying for position.

Ed reluctantly shared his family Christmases and Easters with us. We spent lots of weekends in San Diego. An uneasy tension always pervaded when Jen was around.

It was like Ed was afraid we'd steal Jen back. He didn't know how deeply he was embedded in her heart.

One such weekend she told me that Ed and her dad were a lot alike; men who knew what they wanted and weren't afraid to go after it. She said that was one of the sterling qualities that had attracted her to Ed.

I shared this with Paul and all I got was, "Hrumph!"

On an evening in June the phone rang. "Mom, get Dad on the extension, I have exciting news for you both." I called Paul and while he listened in, Jen talked a mile a minute. "We're being transferred to Japan for three years; isn't that a hoot?"

My heart gave a jump; I stared numbly at the receiver. Japan! *Oh, no, how could Ed take our Jennifer so far away?*

I didn't want to rain on her parade, but let's face it, at that moment Ed wasn't winning any points with either Paul or me. I wondered how Paul felt about this; he hadn't said a word.

Paul feigned an enthusiasm I was sure he didn't feel.

"Well, we'll just have to come visit you," he replied cheerily.

They left for Japan and a funny thing happened. We missed Jen and the children tremendously, but we missed Ed, too. We missed his smile, his personality, and his sense of humor.

Paul and I always listened in on different extensions on our weekly phone calls. One Sunday Jen called so breathless she could hardly speak.

"Mom, Ed got the Sailor of the Year Award!"

"Wow, Jen! What an honor," I replied.

"Yes, and he's getting promoted to officer's school. The Mustang program."

Evidently Paul understood this military jargon, because he was excited.

Then Ed got on the line.

"Hey, you folks will have to come to the ceremony. You two would love Japan. Besides, I would be honored to have you as my guests."

"I think it's time for that visit," my husband replied.

I was surprised, actually shocked. Was this an offer of a truce in the war for Jennifer's heart?

I couldn't take time off from work, but Paul was determined to go. He traveled over five thousand miles for twelve hours to proudly stand beside his son-in-law at the ceremony.

It has been many years since that first night when Ed said, "We're not doing pictures." Paul came home from Japan with over 200 digital photos on his camera. I look at these images of Ed and Paul on either side of Jennifer, both grinning from ear to ear. I guess they both have matured through the years and decided her heart has enough love for both of them.

Sallie Rodman

Not My Father's Son

Those who bring sunshine into the lives of others cannot keep it from themselves.

J. M. Barrie

My father came back from the Army after World War II eager to dive into the American Dream. He had a wife, a young daughter, and plans for the good life. The first thing he planned to do was to buy a Buick. Then he found out that he was going to be a father again.

"Well," he said, "if I can't have a Buick, I'll at least have a son."

When I was born, he very quickly saw that I was a scrawny, squally baby girl. I was not a Buick, and I was not his son.

Whether I sensed this or it was just my biological makeup, I tended toward more boyish activities. While my sister yearned for a Tiny Tears doll, I wanted a hammer of my own. When she played house with her friends, I was busy pretending I was a cowboy riding the range on my white stallion—a long-handled broom with a bristly straw mane. When she went shopping, I went climbing up the back of the neighbor's steep, slanted garage roof to play spy. My sister could whack a Spalding during a punchball game, but I could hit an infield punch that sent the other team scrambling while I ran the bases.

My father let me watch him when he worked around the house, and sometimes he let me help. I loved being my father's assistant on his home improvement projects. I learned how to scrape and wax floors, paint walls, spackle holes. I wrapped sandpaper around a wooden block and sanded the rough ends of the boards my father cut. I drew on the sidewalk with pieces of discarded wallboard instead of the chalk my friends used. My mother said I was a tomboy. I just wanted to know how to fix things.

As I grew, I started to like more girly things like dancing and dressing up, but I still liked that I could feel comfortable around a toolbox.

When my father had a heart attack at eighty, he couldn't do the things he used to, so I pitched in. I helped him set up a new apartment after Mom passed away. I put together a cabinet for his bathroom and assembled a dinette set for his small kitchen. I took him on outings, maneuvering his walker and then his wheelchair into and out of the car so that we could walk around the duck pond together in the spring when the ducklings and goslings hatched, or we would go the local doughnut shop to share a snack and a cup of coffee. The logistics didn't frighten me. My father had taught me to look for a way to work with them.

One day as we were out enjoying the sunny weather, I asked Dad if he was disappointed that he didn't have a son after all. He looked at me in surprise.

"No, I'm not disappointed," he said. "You are the best son I never had—and a wonderful daughter."

I was not my father's son, but at that moment I was his proud child.

Ferida Wolff

The Eulogy

We met when he was eighteen. Michael had driven our daughter Nancy home from the Boston area where they were both college freshmen. "How well do you know this boy?" I had asked Nancy when she announced that she'd snagged a ride home. Like any self-respecting mother, I wanted some credentials on the lad who would be in a car for five or six hours with our baby daughter.

"Oh, Michael's great—you'll like him," Nancy had said all those years ago.

And she was right. I felt an instant affection for this tall, curly-haired young man who not only stayed for dinner that night—he also insisted upon doing the cooking. When Michael went out and purchased a whole fish and prepared it like a French chef, I was smitten. "I *really* like this Michael," I told my husband that day. And secretly, I hoped Nancy did, too. We would observe years of Nancy-Mike friendship followed by the best kind of romance, one that grows out of friendship's roots. And by the time they were twenty-five, Nancy and Mike were engaged. A year later, they were married in our garden.

I watched Michael establish himself in a career on Wall

Street, still a mysterious place to me. But I was thrilled that he'd "apprenticed" with his wonderful grandfather, one of the oldest practitioners on that famous street until Grandpa's death several years ago. Likeable, loving Michael grew up before our eyes, became a fine father of three sons of his own, yet never lost his boyishness.

And I naïvely thought I knew him extremely well, since he'd been part of our lives now for more than twenty years. But recently, I saw Michael in a totally new light. On a day drenched with sunshine, the kind of day that seems meant for beginnings, not endings, I watched our Michael stand up in a funeral home and eulogize his own father, Steve. The man had been ill for months, and because he was himself a physician, he knew too much about his own condition. At first, the leukemia was kept at bay, but in recent times it had advanced at a gallop. And Michael himself surely knew that the end was close at hand during those last hospital visits when a son tried to find ways to say good-bye.

Father-son relationships are as tricky and complex as any, and Michael and his dad's was no exception. Two divorces had punctuated Steve's life, and had surely complicated our son-in-law's world. But during Steve's final days, I sensed that acceptance had flowed from all sides. Even though he'd talked about it, I secretly hoped that Michael wouldn't try to deliver a eulogy at his father's funeral. I worried that this good and generous son-in-law of ours would find it too difficult, too emotionally draining. But in a phone conversation the night before the funeral, it became clear that Michael, his sister, and his stepsister would all be participating. I didn't sleep well that night. I kept thinking of our son-in-law struggling with all those feelings. He's always been the sort with a heart as big and wide as the great outdoors, and I worried that Michael would never be able to get through such a daunting task. Funerals are never predictable. This one surely wasn't.

Michael's eulogy came between those of his two sisters. Unlike Rachel, who was emotional and moving in her remarks, and Laura, who was literary and philosophical, Michael was funny. Wonderfully honest. Even irreverent. And it was perfect. As our son-in-law spoke of his brilliant, difficult, generous, impractical father, murmurs of recognition and affirmation rippled throughout the room. Yes, that was Steve. And so was this. And, oh my, didn't we all remember Steve as a grandfather who would plant huge trampolines in the backyards of his grandchildren's homes—and then run away? Didn't we know that no matter what the subject, he would argue to win? And that he somehow always did? Rachel, Laura, and Michael all got it right. And Steve would be forever etched in memory as the man he was, remembered by the children who loved him and knew him so wisely and well. I know that Michael's dad would have been so proud of all of his children.

And for one mother-in-law who never had any sons of her own, seeing and hearing Michael deliver a eulogy for his father was one of those rare moments when endings and beginnings get smudged and shaken. The boy I had met in our kitchen so many years ago was clearly and strikingly a man. A good man. A wise and strong man. A father and a son—and a son-in-law. On that day, in my head and heart, I dropped the "in-law" label. This was a man I was so proud to claim . . . as a son.

Sally Friedman

"Now, there's no pressure to walk in my footsteps,
son . . . But just for the heck of it,
do you want to try on my shoes?"

5

THE CALL
OF DUTY

*Conscience is the root of all true courage;
if a man would be brave let him obey his
conscience.*

James Freeman Clarke

The Last Game

Dignity does not consist in possessing honors, but in deserving them.

Aristotle

It was the scare of my life. One minute my dad was conducting a sales meeting, the next he was on the way to a hospital after suffering what everyone believed to be a heart attack. A few days later my mom insisted I accompany him to the heart specialist to hear the results. She knew her husband well enough to know he would never tell us if the news was bad. My dad and I breathed a sigh of relief when the doctor told us Dad's heart was fine and that sudden pain he had felt was nothing. "Go celebrate!" he smiled.

I was twenty-nine years old and knew very little about the life of the man who lovingly reared and molded me into the man I had become. For a reason I did not understand, Dad steadfastly refused to talk about his life before I was born. He especially shied away from anything to do with baseball. My father, Gene Moore, was a loving and supportive father in every respect, but he kept the door to his past locked. I didn't know why.

Following the doctor's advice, we drove together to George Diamonds Steak House in Chicago, our favorite restaurant. Dad was talkative, happy, and grinning from ear to ear. Now was the time. I swallowed hard and looked him straight in the eye. "Dad, you never came to any of my baseball games, and you would never play catch with me." I paused and watched his smile dissipate. "I thought I lost you last week, and I don't know anything about your life." It was May 12, 1983. The story I was about to hear would change my life forever.

When he realized that brushing aside my question was not going to work, my dad—for the first time in his life—opened that closed door. Although it was difficult for him at first, the words came more easily as the seconds slid into minutes, and the minutes into hours. The man across the booth was finally unburdening himself of the cross he had borne for so many years.

My dad had been a baseball prodigy from the small town of Sesser, Illinois, where a scout from the Brooklyn Dodgers organization came to watch the young catcher work his magic. The scout signed Gene to play catcher with the Dodgers, but only after getting his parents' permission. You see, my dad was only fifteen years old at the time.

His first season with a farm team was a resounding success, but shortly thereafter, in 1941, the Japanese bombed Pearl Harbor. Like so many young men of his generation, fate had other plans for Gene Moore. The Dodgers advised him to avoid combat by enlisting in the Navy and joining the United States Navy Exhibition Baseball Team. Dad played ball for the soldiers in the Azores and across North Africa, honing his skills and dreaming of the day when he could play in Major League Baseball.

In 1944, while stationed in Norfolk, Virginia, members of the United States Navy Exhibition Baseball Team were roused from their sleep and briefed on their new assignment. On June 4, 1944, a Navy Hunter-Killer task force operating off the coast of West Africa captured and boarded U-505, a German U-boat (submarine). So remarkable a feat, and so immensely valuable the intelligence, the news was hidden from the world until after the war ended. Even the German crew did not know their beloved U-505 had been captured intact. The submarine was towed to Bermuda. The captured crewmen ended up in Camp Ruston in northern Louisiana, where they were sequestered and kept hidden from their fellow POWs, the Red Cross, and even their own families. Gene and his fellow ballplayers dropped their gloves and picked up rifles. Their new job was to guard the fifty-plus crewmen.

Completely bored and unable to play the game he loved, my dad convinced the camp commander to let him and his teammates teach the enemy how to play baseball. As he explained it, his unauthorized chats with the Germans convinced him they had a lot in common and could overcome their differences by playing baseball.

And so it came to pass that American baseball players doing time in the Navy and German POWs doing time behind barbed wire learned how to coexist on a baseball diamond. Somewhere along the way, they became friends. The erstwhile enemies played their games outside the wire while other guards, prisoners, and even civilians from the local area gathered to watch and encourage the competitive, and occasionally fiery, competition. When the war ended, my dad planned a final Friendship Game. In a freak incident, Gene Moore suffered an injury that altered the course of his life forever.

In another unusual twist of fate, an offer arrived for my dad to report for spring training with the Pittsburgh Pirates organization. My dad took it, but not for the reasons one might expect. His brief return to the game had an altogether different purpose, one that demonstrated the deep selfless character of the man who would one day be my father. The ending of that storyline made me break out in tears.

My dad was asked to spring training in 1949 by the Pittsburgh Pirates affiliate in Greenville, Mississippi, to help a former pitcher-teammate move up to the next level. The pitcher threw a forkball that was difficult to catch, and my dad was one of the few who could catch it. The Pirates made him an offer in order to support the struggling pitcher. My dad reported to Greenville, and when the pitcher moved up, my father was released and sent home.

My father carried with him to the grave the deep pain and aching disappointment of not making it to the majors. He was always grateful that the Pirates had given him a second opportunity to make it, but he also knew that his injury was too severe to overcome. He lived the rest of his life knowing that his time teaching German POWs to play baseball changed his life forever.

After our hours-long conversation concluded, we ended our night together. I could hardly wait until the next day so we could pick up where we left off. My head was spinning with questions begging for an answer. But God had other plans. The doctor was wrong. My dad died of a massive heart attack that next afternoon. He was fifty-seven years old.

I spent twenty years struggling with the untimely death of my dad and the story he had shared less than twenty-four hours before leaving us. To my surprise, my mom knew Dad's story intimately. She was the only one he shared his story with. Other than my mom and those who had known him as a young man, no one knew the story of Gene Moore, the prodigy from Sesser who could hit the ball a country mile and throw grown men out at second base without even standing up.

As far as Dad was concerned, he had been born to play baseball, and the heartbreak he suffered with the loss of his career was nearly unbearable for him. Although he never came to grips with what God had planned for him, he went on to build a wonderful life as a husband, father, and successful businessman. Gene Moore was like so many other American vets who went to war, returned, then shoved that chapter of their lives behind a door they rarely opened. His was not the horrors of combat, but the loss of his identity—of all he believed he was. But to me, the son, the moral of my dad's story was clear: it is not the destination of this great journey that is important, but who we become as we move toward our dream.

My mom never remarried. "I only ever loved one man and that was enough for me," she said. One day, I mentioned in passing that I wanted to write Dad's story to share with their grandkids. "But do I have the right to tell a story Dad did not share himself?" I asked her.

Mom smiled and replied, "Just because he did not talk about himself did not mean he did not love it when others did. Write his story, Gary."

Life is indeed often stranger than fiction. My dad never made it to the major leagues, and he never experienced the stardom and notoriety that come with being a celebrity. But today, people all over the world are finally learning about the story of the teenage baseball legend from Sessser destined for stardom until a hand touched him on the shoulder and turned him in a different direction. If not for the first nonfatal heart attack and the faulty diagnosis, I would never have learned about my dad's life before I was born.

Gene may have played his last game in 1949 and left us twenty-four years ago, but his story of character, destiny, and what a man does with a second chance has truly become a conversation between generations.

Gary W. Moore

[AUTHOR'S NOTE: *Those words catapulted me into action. As a result, I wrote the award-winning book* Playing with the Enemy: A Baseball Prodigy, a World at War and a Field of Broken Dreams *(Savas Beatie, 2006). Gene's story profoundly and positively influenced lives across the country. Everyone has broken dreams and how we deal with them makes us who we are today.* Playing with the Enemy *inspired readers to write hundreds of letters, create moving poetry, and write songs about the boy from Sesser and his love of the game. People now drive hundreds of miles to visit the small town of Sesser, where my dad learned to play ball at "The Lumberyard," and returned to seek solace when his world turned upside down.*

This story took another amazing twist recently. Academy Award–winning producer Gerald Molen purchased the rights to my dad's story, which will soon be a major motion picture. He selected a young Hollywood up-and-comer named Toby Moore to play the role of Gene. It is a combination unlike any in Hollywood history. I wrote a book about my father, and the handsome young man who will play the role of Gene is my son, Toby Moore.]

Jumping the Generation Gap

"Steven, now that we've arrived for another summer on our Missouri farm, remember that country living is different from our city life in Florida," Jim said as he slammed the hood of the old pickup, wiped his greasy hands on a rag, and continued talking to our son, while I stood nearby. "You'll be around farm equipment and you need to practice safety."

"I'll be careful, Dad. And now that I'm thirteen will you and Mom let me buy a dirt bike with the money I've earned?"

Jim glanced at me and I nodded my approval. "Okay, son. We can look for a dirt bike tomorrow morning. We'll drive to that motorcycle shop fifty miles north of here and see what they have."

"Thanks, Mom and Dad!" said our grateful son as he embraced me and beamed at his father.

The next afternoon Jim and Steven returned with a black and yellow dirt bike perched in the back of the pickup.

"Look, Mom!" Steven exclaimed as he leaped into the truck bed and sat on the bike's seat. "Isn't this cool? Some kid just outgrew it. We got a good deal! I'm going to go ride this cool machine!"

"Hold on!" interrupted Jim. "This bike is new to you. Let's spend some time checking it out and talking about safety."

When the guys finished going over the bike and basic safety rules, Steven cranked the motor that sounded like a chain saw. Then our son raced across the pasture on his new toy.

"Is the bike dangerous? Are we being too lenient as parents? Will he take risks?" I asked my husband.

"He's got a good head on his shoulders, and I've taught him to be careful," said Jim as the sound of the bike faded into a distant pasture.

Steven was thrilled with his bike. He rode it every day, stopping long enough to coax his dad into driving him to the only gas station in the area to fill five-gallon cans.

Steven's friend Scott, who lived in town, decided he, too, wanted a dirt bike and coaxed his dad into buying one. The two boys raced their little motorcycles in the pastures and along roads. When the summer rains arrived, the country roads became muddy and slippery.

"Watch out for these slick roads," Jim warned. "That mud can get the best of you and take your bike down in a minute."

"I'll be careful," Steven promised.

The rains continued, and the creeks began to rise. Torrents of water rushed under the one-lane wooden bridge that connected our farm to the town. At a break in the weather, Steven said, "I'm going into town to visit Scott. See you later!"

The setting sun was turning the sky a dusty orange when Steven returned and entered the kitchen.

"How's Scott?" I inquired.

"Fine," he replied as he grabbed a chocolate chip cookie and sat at the table next to his dad.

"Any news from town?" Jim asked.

"Yeah, the wooden bridge is out. The high creek washed it away!"

"That's terrible news," said Jim. "They'll have to rebuild it right away. We can't get to town without a bridge."

"I did," mumbled Steven.

"You did?" asked Jim, looking puzzled. "That's impossible! If the bridge is out, there's no way to cross over that stream."

"Yes, there is."

"How?" I asked.

"On my bike! It was awesome!"

"Don't tell me you jumped your dirt bike over that raging water! You could have been killed!" said his agitated father.

"But, Dad, I wasn't killed. I had no choice! It was fantastic! I just backed my bike up a few feet. Then when I got to the stream I gunned the engine, and my bike flew into the air and landed on the other side! While I was in the air I worried for a second that I wouldn't make it, but I landed okay. When I told Scott about it, he was jealous."

"Oh, Steven!" I moaned. "I can't believe you did that! How did you get back home? Don't tell me you . . ."

"The same way! It was even better the second time! I'll never forget it!"

"What you did was risky and unsafe!" said Jim. "You're lucky you weren't injured or killed. After all our talks about safety, you made a bad decision."

Summers passed. Steven graduated from the Coast Guard Academy and no longer joined us on the farm. Then an eventful day arrived.

Before noon a father and his young son came to test-drive the dirt bike we advertised in the rural paper. The boy zoomed along the gravel road. When he drove back to the farmhouse, his face was flushed with excitement.

"You'll have to be careful on that thing," his dad warned

as he took out his wallet and handed Jim some bills. He waved as they drove away with the dirt bike bouncing in the back of the truck.

Jim and I got in our old pickup and headed to town. We stopped at the wooden bridge that was rebuilt when the stream washed away the old one years ago.

"After all my lectures on safety, Steven fearlessly jumped his dirt bike across this stream and survived," said Jim. Then a smile played at the corners of his mouth, and he added, "I have to admit, when I was an adventuresome kid his age, I would have done the same thing. Now that Steven is a Coast Guard Officer, risking his life to save people from dangerous waters, perhaps his jumping a swollen stream on his dirt bike was practice for his future career."

Miriam Hill

Reunion

Call it a clan, call it a network, call it a tribe, call it a family. Whatever you call it, whoever you are, you need one.

Jane Howard

The last time I had seen Dad was at Aberdeen Proving Grounds in Maryland, when he came down from Washington to give me my first salute as a brand-new second lieutenant. Dad had gone from War Production Board to the Navy's Military Government School. Why the Navy, when his four sons were in the Army in places such as North Africa and London? He was always competing with his brood, and this was his way of being "a little bit better."

A lot of water had passed under the bridge in the year following that first salute. Dad shipped out to Okinawa as second-in-command of military government on that heavily fought-over island. I volunteered for the Bomb Disposal School and, sometime after that six-week course, flew to the Philippines to join the war. My older brother, Joe, went on to the Anzio Beachhead, Royal married a Red

Cross worker, and my youngest brother, Bill, went with the OSS (Office of Strategic Services) to England. My wife, Julie, was pregnant with our second child, who, some twenty years later, would join the Army (like his dear old dad) during the Vietnam War.

So . . . no chance to catch up with any of my brothers, but what about the guy who gave me my first salute? He was a mere 800 to 1000 miles away from my post in Batanga, Luzon. Could I drop in on Dad and return the salute? I would try.

A bomb disposal squad consisted of an officer and six noncommissioned officers, and was always attached to a larger unit for rations and quarters. I looked up the battalion commanding officer, a good guy, and persuaded him that all of the unexploded bombs and artillery shells found for us each day by G-2 would still be waiting to be defused or blown up on my return.

The colonel agreed to give me travel orders to legitimize my planned junket. The orders, handwritten on the back of an envelope, simply said, "It is o.k. for Lt. Firman to be absent from his post for a week beginning August 17."

A member of my squad drove me to Manila where I found space on a troop carrier flying to Okinawa. Arriving there a few hours later, I worked my way via thumb to military headquarters, skirting the Japanese lines en route.

Headquarters: Quonset huts surrounded by trimmed lawns and beds of bright flowers, and officers dressed in neatly pressed Navy gray uniforms. And I? Wearing wrinkled suntans, combat boots, a beat-up cap, and packing a .45 pistol on my hip. In addition, I was yellow from Atabrine, a malaria suppressant, and I was sporting a large mustache.

I peeked in, and seeing Dad sitting there, I walked up to his desk and said, "Don't get up; this is an informal visit."

He looked up at this stranger, a mere lieutenant telling

a full commander not to get up. His face got red and I almost saw smoke coming out of his ears as he looked for a shore patrolman to take this lunatic away.

But as he began to recognize my features, he said, "Is that you, Win?" Surprise, laughter, hugging, and we began a three-day mini-reunion with the war going on around us. My plan worked so well that the visit became the high point of the whole blinking war for me and my dad.

Win Firman

Semper Fi

Act with courage, and may the Lord be with those who do well.

2 Chronicles 19:11b (NIV)

The call came on a scorching Saturday afternoon. Our younger son Rick, stationed at Cherry Point Marine Corps Air Station in North Carolina, had been admitted to the hospital with a ruptured appendix. "They brought him down to Camp Lejeune and performed surgery," his friend reported, "but I can't find him."

Fear took over. A ruptured appendix can prove fatal. "We'll be there as soon as we can," I said, "but we're two states away." *Oh, God, please help Rick.*

I called my husband, Joe, in from mowing the lawn and, frantic, he phoned Camp Lejeune, locating the surgeon. "Yes, I operated on your son this morning," he said. "The infection had spread into the surrounding tissues. We're leaving the incision open in case we have to go back in there." *That means peritonitis has set in. Lord, help.* My courage just vanished . . .

"I have to tell you," the doctor added, "he is a very sick

boy. But he's young; he's in good physical shape. I think he'll be able to make it." *Oh, Lord, give us all courage and strength.*

Joe never talks while driving, so I had practically all night to think—and worry.

Why in the world had Rick waited so long before seeing a doctor? Then my wandering mind reasoned: *Why am I surprised? The Marine Corps evidently teaches its men they can withstand anything—that they're invincible.*

I should know. Joe is a Marine to the core. *Semper Fidelis*—"always faithful." He had enlisted at age seventeen, served on Guam, Japan, and China, and now, with the rank of major, met with a reserve unit in Atlanta.

On the open road this night, the steady drone of the car engine provided the only sound. Soon we were swallowed up in blackness, blackness relieved only by the streetlights of an occasional town, sleeping now.

Continuing my reverie, I contemplated the crucial factor that had influenced Rick, affected us all for that matter. Four years earlier, we had faced another surgical crisis when Joe was diagnosed with incurable cancer. Although he appeared to be beating the odds, the outcome as yet was uncertain. He had been demoralized when the Marine Corps declared him medically unfit to serve. Just recently, though, he had been reinstated to active status and even dared to hope for a promotion in rank.

The fact that Rick followed his dad's example shouldn't have surprised me.

The specter of uncertainty about his dad's health clouded the years Rick was in college. The week of graduation, he had his hair cut short, shaved off his beard, and joined the corps. "Somebody's got to carry on the tradition," he had explained.

Joe and I reached Camp Lejeune at three o'clock in the morning and located the hospital, a soon-to-be-replaced red brick building of World War I vintage, three stories, dark now except for a smattering of dim lights on each floor.

Inside, our footsteps echoed down dismal hallways. A squeaky elevator emptied us onto the third floor where a small lamp revealed a desk and a nurse bent over her paperwork. We asked her about our son.

"Would you like to see him?"

"Oh, yes! May we?"

"Follow me," she said. With a flashlight, she cut a path down the black asphalt-tiled floor of yet another gloomy corridor.

"He's in the room with another patient," the nurse said softly, motioning us through a door.

"We'll need to be as quiet as possible."

We could barely detect Rick's bed in the shadows. Following the sounds of muted groans, being careful of the IV-dispensing contraption with its tubes and bottles, I touched his shoulder. His hospital gown was drenched with perspiration. "Rick," I whispered, bending close to his ear, "it's Mother and Dad."

A very groggy son answered, "I'm glad you're here."

I kissed his fevered brow, "I love you."

"Love you, too," he managed, then drifted back into a medicine-induced sleep.

Lord, our boy here needs your healing touch. And, Lord, about that courage—I need it now, really badly.

Rick was alert the next day but still feverish and miserable with pain.

On Monday morning, Joe let me out at the front door to the hospital while he found a parking space. The hallways, quiet all weekend, bustled now with activity. White-uniformed nurses and corpsmen hurried in and out of rooms; patients—all wearing U.S. Navy–issued blue cotton robes and scuffs—did their prescribed walking.

When I reached Rick's room, he lay flat on his back, anxiously eyeing the door. "Where's Dad?" he asked hurriedly, a note of excitement in his voice.

"He's parking the car."

"Can you help me get up?" he said, painfully pushing the sheet back with his feet and with great effort raising himself on one elbow. "I've got to be standing when Dad gets here."

I sensed this was no time for questions. Taking his arms while he clenched his teeth against the pain, I pulled him around into a sitting position on the edge of the bed, then sat down beside him. While he held his incision with one hand, he placed the other one around my shoulder. I, in turn, put one arm around his back, with my other hand steadying us with his IV pole. Somehow we stood to the floor and propped the back of his legs against the bed. Then he motioned me to ease away.

Just in time. Masculine footsteps in the hall. Joe barely got inside the room when he stopped in his tracks, not believing what he saw: Rick standing by his bed. Whereupon Rick pulled himself to almost-full height, snapped to attention, and with a crisp salute, heralded, "Congratulations, Colonel, Sir!"

"Wha—wha—what?" Joe stammered, totally bewildered.

"Your promotion came through!" Rick reported, a big grin forming. "Colonel Asher called this morning from Atlanta. You're a lieutenant colonel!"

"Promotion? Called here? How did he find me here?"

To describe Joe as dumbfounded would be a gross understatement. He was undone! Oh, but for a video camera to record the event. Suddenly, it all sank in and his face lit up like the fourth of July!

And just as suddenly, the Marine in him sprang back to life. With his officer demeanor engaged, he "snapped to" and—even though he was wearing civilian clothes, which ruled out an official salute—returned Rick a quick, informal one. "Thank you, Lieutenant."

Then with two long strides, Joe reached Rick and enfolded him in a giant bear hug. I joined in to make it a threesome. We laughed and cried, all at the same time, realizing that probably no promotion had ever come at a more tender moment.

After we helped Rick back into bed, he provided a perfect finish to the stirring scene. Reverting to his affectionate title for his dad, he said, "We're awfully proud of you, Pa."

Pa, the new colonel. We were "just family" once again.

Yet a changed family. For etched forever on my heart is the picture of that young, feverish Marine in a wrinkled, bobtailed hospital gown, barely able to stand, snapping to attention and "promoting" his dad! What a memorable moment! What courage. What strength.

An answer to my prayers—
And *Semper Fi*—to the core.

Gloria Cassity Stargel

"What would a tree fort be without a cannon?"

Squeals and Squeezes

I don't know what your destiny will be, but one thing I do know: the only ones among you who will be really happy are those who have sought and found how to serve.

Albert Schweitzer

I watched a toddler run on sturdy, chubby legs, squealing as he traversed the length of the country club lounge. A tall, good-looking man strode purposefully behind him, closing in on his prey. He reached for the runaway boy with a large hand and grasped nothing but air. The child had spied a banquet table draped in a white linen skirt, and with lightning speed, he'd lifted the cloth and scooted underneath, then turned eerily silent. He knew this hide-and-seek game well, despite his young age.

The dad circled the table with one ear cocked, waiting for his son to reveal his whereabouts. After two full circles, he leaned down, picked up the cloth and peered underneath. The little boy giggled and squealed as his daddy grabbed hold of him, scooped him into his arms, and held him close. The little boy pulled back and gazed straight into his daddy's eyes. Not a word was said, but the child wound both arms around his daddy's neck and squeezed, then lay his blond head on the man's broad shoulder. The dad held the child close to his heart, kissed his cheek, then stroked his hair as he carried him back to the gathering of families nearby.

I felt privileged to watch these two, for I'd witnessed a simple moment of a father and son at play. It proved to be a scene that etched itself onto my heart, a forever memory. The daddy was a member of an Army attack battalion stationed at an Army post near our town. He'd served a tour in Iraq, and in a matter of weeks, he'd board a transport plane with his battalion and return to the battlefield once again. But now, he and his family were attending a recognition dinner at our country club. On this night, he wasn't a soldier wearing full body armor, clutching his rifle—on the alert for any strange movements or sounds. Tonight he could be a daddy playing with a child he loved. He'd already missed a full year of the boy's growing up, and all too soon, he'd be gone again. *How much more would he miss? Who would play "catch me" with the boy while he was gone?*

Once he's back in Iraq, the young soldier might lie in his bunk at night, too weary to sleep. His thoughts will no doubt turn to home, his wife, and his energetic, playful son. The boy will be talking in sentences by the time this tour ends. And pretty soon he'll be old enough to play catch in the backyard. A boy needs a dad to get him ready for his first baseball team.

I have a feeling this father will replay the evening's chase in his mind myriad times. More than a game; it was yet another link in the bonding between father and son. The squeals and squeezes of both translate easily into love a father has for a son in its purest form. I pray that love survives the separation and renews itself with more squeals and squeezes when the soldier-daddy comes home again.

Nancy Julien Kopp

One Child, Many Parents

It takes a village to raise a child.

African Proverb

If my husband, Steve Moreau, had lived, I'm pretty sure he'd be astounded by how much our son, Matt, looks like him. Obviously, Steve left his genetic calling card—so some traits were bound to travel via an invisible in utero father-to-son handshake. Matt has the same blue eyes, same square jaw, same lanky frame. Matt's smile creates dimples in the exact same location on his cheek as his father's, and his posture is a mirror image of the man who once towered above me.

He'd be proud, I'm sure, that the Moreau genes trumped all others, and I believe he would have spent the last eighteen years reminding me of this fact. Father and son barely had eight months together, and yet somehow Matt managed to acquire the same troubled squint and an identical laugh. He never saw his father row, but his love of the sport is the same. Both Steve and Matt loved the sound of eight oars slicing the water and the slow burn that comes from pushing past the pain. Matt is his father's son in so many ways. However, the best things about Matt, the things that Steve would be the proudest of, are the things he didn't live long enough to teach his boy.

The year Steve died, 1987, was a bad year for the Moreau family. Three days after Matt was born, Steve's father died suddenly. Eight months later, the Navy jet Steve was flying crashed in the desert. Any other family might have drowned in their individual sorrows. But the Moreaus aren't just family—this is a family of unspeakable strength. They stepped in and became for Matt every aspect of the father they knew Steve would have wanted to him to have. They started with the "dad basics": how to build a fire, how to rock climb, how to surf—things Steve would have loved doing with Matt. But they also let Matt discover the best of himself by helping him embrace a man in death who wasn't perfect in life. Steve's brothers and sisters knew all of Steve's stories—the good and the bad, the triumphant and embarrassing. They never failed to share with Matt that his father was human, that he made mistakes and had regrets, but these mistakes built character. It's been through Matt's own character-building moments that he learned how to dig deep and push himself when he wanted to give up. When he falls, he gets up and finds another way because his aunts and uncles taught him the meaning of sacrifice. Because their moral compass was strong, Matt learned to require more of himself every day. Their joy in the saddest of times taught Matt to laugh at himself and appreciate the opportunities he's been given.

Steve would be proud of how far Matt has come, how hard he has worked, what he's accomplished, and how bravely he has fought to grow up in the image of a father whom he adored. It turns out, Steve's absence didn't make Matt less of a man, it made him a stronger one. I think we can all be proud of that.

Melissa Moreau Baumann

An Understanding

To protect those who are not able to protect themselves is a duty which every one owes to society.

Edward Macnaghten

When I was younger, I could never understand one thing about my father. Every December, he would watch the movie *Tora! Tora! Tora!* and his eyes would fill with tears. I remember asking him about it once, why it bothered him so, but as hard as he tried to explain it to me, I could not understand. I knew the movie was about the attack on Pearl Harbor and that hundreds of people had died in the attack, but not why it bothered him so badly. To me, it was something to be studied in the history books. It happened, we went to war, and won. That's all I could understand of it.

I joined the Navy in 1985, six years after my father had died. You could say I followed in his footsteps. He served in 1955. I've made the Navy my career and am stationed on the USS *George Washington,* an aircraft carrier. I started to understand my father's tears when we were on a training cruise for four days. We left on September 10, 2001. The

next day, everything came to a standstill for a few hours
as we watched in horror what was happening. We are
lucky enough to get satellite TV, and we stayed glued to
CNN until we started landing aircraft. I didn't have much
time to think that day—or to feel. My job was to get the
names, next of kin information, and embark all these
people coming on board.

September 12, I truly understood why my father's eyes
would well up with tears. We were the assigned flagship
over the ships that scrambled underway to protect our
nation. Before we went on station, we were given one mission that was essential, some would call it a "Show the
Flag" mission, but it was the most important mission I'd
ever been on. I stood in our forward hanger bay looking
out of the bay door as we cruised through New York
Harbor. In the distance, I could see the smoke still rising
where the World Trade Center used to stand. Around me,
others watched also, many crying.

When we returned to port on September 17, it was to a
different world, a different country. I had heard about the
changes already in effect from people coming aboard and
from my wife as well. When I got home I sat and read the
papers dated September 12. It was then that I understood
why my father felt so emotional about that day in
December when he was eight. Young as he was, he knew
that innocent people had died. He knew that the safety he
had taken for granted was at risk. As I write this, I am
deployed in support of Operation Enduring Freedom, the
War on Terror, if you will, and I think of my son, eleven
years old. I don't know if I can explain to him how I feel,
though I'll try. I hope that when he is older, he doesn't
have to learn to understand through tragedies as great as
Pearl Harbor or the terrorist attacks of September 11. But I
know his sense of a safe world has been shaken, too.

Those of us who serve do so in hopes of creating that

safe world for our children. Our ship received a gift from a local school: a garland made of construction paper on which children wrote words of encouragement. One said, "Thanks for letting my little sister grow up in a peaceful country." I now know how my father felt that day in 1941. But I can't bring myself to watch the movie. I've lived it myself. I wish my father were here so I could tell him I finally understand. I think he knows, because every so often over the years I've felt his presence near. September 11 was one of them.

Robert Anderson

Lessons from My Father

You don't raise heroes, you raise sons. And if you treat them like sons they'll turn out to be heroes, even if it's just in your own eyes.

Walter M. Schirra

It was a day that held more emotion than any other in the nineteen years before it. The day spent with my son made me so proud; then a short while later, the trip home was very hard to bear.

Our youngest son, Tim, wanted to join the Army shortly after his nineteenth birthday. He asked if I would take him down to the recruiting station, saying I could watch him being sworn in if I wanted. I told him I wouldn't miss it for anything in the world.

The trip to the recruiting office was over before we knew it. Time had passed through our hands quickly as I tried to tell him every important thing (at least to me) I could think of. After we arrived and Tim was checked in, we learned the meaning of "hurry up and wait." We were told it would be a while before the ceremony would begin. Tim and I decided to wait in the main auditorium. The room held thirty to forty men and women. Most were close to the same age as Tim, and most, like us, were waiting.

A young lady sat down by Tim and struck up a conversation, asking where he was from and where he was going. Tim answered her questions and then introduced her to me. She said she wished her mom had come, telling us how they had gotten into a big fight before she left home. It was about her joining the Army. Her voice sounded very dry and rough, and I knew they hadn't parted on the best of terms. She needed someone to be proud of her. I wish I would have told her how proud I was, but it was not the right place to tell her. The wait ended, and before we knew it, the new recruits were taken into a small room for their swearing in. Not as many parents were there as I expected, but I was proud to be able to join the group as an observer. The commander explained the swearing in and the oath they were about to take, asking the soldiers if they were there of their own free will. All answered, "Yes, sir!" He then asked the group to hold up their right hands and repeat the vow to serve our country.

As I looked at each soldier, every one of them meant every word—every word! The service took my breath away. These young men and women knew what they had just committed to do. I kept saying to myself, *Dear Lord, give them strength!*

After the group was released, many, like Tim and I, took a few photos. It was those photos that would help carry us for the next eight weeks. We would not be able to see him again until his graduation from boot camp at Fort Knox, Kentucky. Tim walked me out to the car and we said our good-byes.

The ride home was one of the longest of my life. Being all alone with my memories was the hardest part of this day, and one of the toughest moments of my life. I felt like I had just given away my son. Question after question filled my mind. *Had we taught him all he needed to know? Had he listened? What is he going to be like when he is all done? Did he know how much his mom and I loved him?* This was my little boy! We watched him grow up. Now, suddenly, he wasn't ours anymore. Yes, he was still part of our family, but we no longer helped control his decisions. Tim was still our youngest son, but no longer our little boy. Today, he was quickly becoming a man.

It wasn't until after Tim arrived in Iraq, six months later, that I would get the answer to several of the questions that had filled my mind on the long road home from the recruiting office. The answers came through an e-mail Tim had sent me at work:

Hey, Dad, I got a special coin today from our Lt. Colonel for fixing a generator while we were on a three-day mission. We had mechanics who couldn't even fix it, so I stepped up and said I would try. I found the bad wiring under the control panel and fixed it. It started right up! They asked how I knew how to do that, and I told them my dad was a mechanic. My sergeant said, Well, I guess he taught you well. So I just wanted to say, "thank you" for always making me stand out there and help whenever something broke, even though I really didn't want to. I guess they really needed that generator so we could continue on our mission; so fixing it was a big deal. That is why they gave me the coin. This is also a big deal because I'm only the third one in my company to get one of these coins. Well, I just wanted to tell you that I miss you and I hope things are going good. Love, Tim

I sat at my desk thinking about the many lessons my father had taught me. I smiled remembering how he was never afraid to try to fix anything, and he, too, always encouraged our help. Today the lessons from my father worked through the hands of my son, a half a world away, and I have never been prouder.

William Garvey

Leadership, Whose Way?

If you think you can, you can; if you think you can't, you're right.

Mary Kay Ash

I arrived as a new, nineteen-year-old second lieutenant in the Philippines soon after WWII ended. It was my responsibility to support my mother, my thirteen-year-old sister, and my five-year-old brother. My dad had moved out just as I graduated from high school.

I was in charge of sixty-two men in my platoon. Our assignment was to do geodesic surveying in the jungle to produce better maps. Since my immediate superior was far away in Manila, I felt the weight of total responsibility not only for surveying accuracy, but also for the safety, food, and shelter of my men.

To top it off, I had a big problem. I'd just returned from a "leadership meeting" in Manila, where the colonel taught what seemed wrong to me. He ordered, "Command, don't ask, a man to do something. Don't ask for advice from anyone, not even your platoon sergeant. That shows your weakness. Never admit a mistake. You wouldn't be an officer if you weren't better than your men. So act it!"

I had been leading my platoon with the exact opposite style of leadership. My dad, an infantry major, had taught me "Your job is not to command; your job is to lead. Get all the input you can from everyone. Have the courage to admit an honest mistake. Be tough, but be fair. Above all, earn your men's respect so they can have confidence in you."

My dad had let me down hard by leaving our family in my care, and the Manila colonel obviously had a lot of experience. Should I change my style of leadership from what Dad had taught me?

Then there was an older man, Randall, busted from staff sergeant to private just before he was transferred to me. He had a surly attitude to go with his tough body and big mouth. He did everything he could think of to make my men lose confidence in me.

My platoon and I had just finished a tough job. We were all tired, dirty, and short of water, which was a heyday for Randall's putting me down to the men.

I sent Andy, the red-haired sergeant of the second squad, to look for water along the road we planned to take. When Andy returned, he reported that he had found water and even recommended a swim at the river he'd found during his reconnaissance. I said, "Great!"

Less than a city block to the river, which was hidden by dense jungle, he'd found a delightful place. The river was relatively wide with a semblance of beaches on the far side and a rock cliff on our side.

After swimming, my sergeants—including red-haired Andy—and I were taking turns "life guarding" from on top of the cliff eighteen feet above the river, when Randall started yelling. "Lieutenant Hill, show us how you can dive!" The cliff was twice as high as the nine-foot diving board at my city pool, and my dives from it hadn't been pretty. So I just ignored him.

"Lieutenant Hill, can't you hear me? Lieutenant Hill, if you don't dive, I'll have to come up and throw you off. You don't have your bars on now, *sir*, so you *are* fair game!"

Oh, why hadn't I just dived? The knots in my stomach didn't help as I stood up to meet him as he came up the cliff. To me he looked like a giant. As a youth I had been particularly small, so I had focused on wrestling to take care of myself.

Randall looked surprised when I grabbed his right arm and thrust out my left leg as he lunged at me. As he tripped over my leg, I saw him sail over the cliff. When he came up out of the river, the whole platoon was laughing uproariously . . . all but Randall.

Back up to the top of the cliff he came, face red as fire, hate in his eyes. As we crashed together, I got my left foot behind his right leg and came across with my right arm, elbow cocked. Down he went again! This time it was deathly quiet as Randall came at a dead run out of the water, swearing at the top of his lungs. I thought, *I've had it.* So when we collided, I flung my arms around him and hung on tight. As he pulled me off my feet, I wrapped my legs around him. If I went, he was coming with me! I saw his cocked fist—aimed at my nose.

Red-haired Andy, who had been lying on the cliff, had slid closer and planted both of his feet on us, his knees flexed. He let out a war whoop, straightened his legs, and I felt myself falling with Randall. We let go of each other and inverted, making headfirst dives into the water.

As I came up, I couldn't help but laugh. And Randall? He started laughing, too. "Somebody pushed us!" The whole platoon cheered, and in that mad moment, Randall and I shook hands. It was a wonderful feeling—one that lasted—and it sure convinced me that my dad's style of leadership was the right one after all.

Somehow I had carried the best of Dad within me. And knowing that he had guided me wisely was the beginning of the healing of our father-son relationship.

Louis A. Hill, Jr.

The Boys of Iwo Jima

Strong reasons make strong actions.

Shakespeare

Each year my video production company is hired to go to Washington, DC, with the eighth-grade class from Clinton, Wisconsin, where I grew up, to videotape their trip. I always enjoy visiting our nation's capital, and each year I take some special memories back with me. But this fall's trip was especially memorable.

On the last night of our trip, we stopped at the Iwo Jima Memorial. It is the largest bronze statue in the world and depicts one of the most famous photographs in history— the World War II image of the six brave men raising the American flag at the top of Mount Suribachi on the island of Iwo Jima, Japan. About one hundred students and chaperones piled off the buses and headed toward the memorial. I noticed a solitary figure at the base of the statue, and as I got closer, he asked, "What's your name, and where are you guys from?"

I told him that my name was Michael Powers and that we were from Clinton, Wisconsin.

"Hey, I'm a Cheesehead, too! Come gather around, Cheeseheads, and I will tell you a story."

James Bradley just happened to be in Washington, DC, to speak at the memorial the following day. He was there that night to say good night to his dad, who had previously passed away, but whose image is part of the statue. He was just about to leave when he saw the buses pull up. I videotaped him as he spoke to us, and received his permission to share what he said from my videotape. It is one thing to tour the incredible monuments depicting great moments in history, but it is quite another to get the kind of insight we received that night. When all had gathered around, he reverently began to speak.

"My name is James Bradley, and I'm from Antigo, Wisconsin. My dad is on that statue, and I just wrote a book called *Flags of Our Fathers,* which is number five on the *New York Times* bestseller list right now. It is the story of the six boys you see behind me. Six boys raised the flag."

That's when he pointed to the guy putting the pole into the ground and told us his name was Harlon Block. "Harlon was an all-state football player. He enlisted in the Marine Corps with all the senior members of his football team. They were off to play another type of game, a game called 'war.' But it didn't turn out to be a game. Harlon, at the age of twenty-one, died with his intestines in his hands."

Bradley shared that detail with us because he said that people stand in front of the statue and talk about the glory of war. "You guys need to know that most of the boys in Iwo Jima were seventeen, eighteen, and nineteen years old."

He pointed again to the statue. "You see this next guy? That's Rene Gagnon from New Hampshire. If you took Rene's helmet off at the moment this photo was taken, you would find a photograph in the webbing. A photograph of his girlfriend. Rene put that in there for protection, because he was scared. He was eighteen years old. Boys won the battle of Iwo Jima. Boys. Not men."

The next image on the statue was that of Sergeant Mike Strank, we learned. "Mike is my hero," Bradley exclaimed. "He was the hero of all these guys. They called him the 'old man' because he was so old. He was already twenty-four. When Mike would motivate his boys in training camp, he didn't say, 'Let's go kill the enemy' or 'Let's die for our country.' He knew he was talking to little boys. Instead he would say, 'You do what I say, and I'll get you home to your mothers.' "

The next man on the statue was Ira Hayes, a Pima Indian from Arizona who lived through the terror of Iwo Jima. "Ira Hayes walked off Iwo Jima. He went into the White House with my dad, and President Truman told him, 'You're a hero.' He told reporters, 'How can I feel like a hero when two hundred and fifty of my buddies hit the island with me and only twenty-seven of us walked off alive?'

"So, you take your class at school. Two hundred and fifty of you spending a year together having fun, doing everything together. Then all two hundred and fifty of you hit the beach, but only twenty-seven of your classmates walk off alive. That was Ira Hayes. He had images of horror in his mind."

We learned that Ira Hayes died dead drunk, facedown at the age of thirty-two, ten years after the famous photo was taken.

"The next guy, going around the statue, is Franklin Sousley from Hilltop, Kentucky; a fun-lovin' hillbilly boy," Bradley continued. "Franklin died on Iwo Jima at the age of nineteen. When the telegram came to tell his mother that he was dead, it went to the Hilltop General Store. A barefoot boy ran that telegram up to his mother's farm. The neighbors could hear her scream all night and into the morning. The neighbors lived a quarter of a mile away."

Finally, Bradley pointed to the statue's image of his father, John Bradley, from Antigo, Wisconsin. His dad lived until 1994, but had declined all interviews. "When Walter Kronkite or the *New York Times* would call, we were trained as little kids to say, 'No, I'm sorry, sir, my dad's not here. He is in Canada fishing. No, there is no phone there, sir. No, we don't know when he is coming back.' My dad never fished or even went to Canada. Usually he was sitting right there at the table eating his Campbell's soup, but we had to tell the press that he was out fishing. He didn't want to talk to the press. You see, my dad didn't see himself as a hero. Everyone thinks these guys are heroes, 'cause they are in a photo and a monument. My dad knew better. He was a medic. John Bradley from Wisconsin was a caregiver. In Iwo Jima he probably held over two hundred boys as they died, and when boys died in Iwo Jima, they writhed and screamed in pain."

Bradley recalled his third-grade teacher calling the elder Bradley a hero. "When I went home and told my dad that, he looked at me and said, 'I want you always to remember that the heroes of Iwo Jima are the guys who did not come back. *Did not come back.*'

"So, that's the story about six nice young boys," Bradley finished. "Three died on Iwo Jima, and three came back as national heroes. Overall, seven thousand boys died on Iwo Jima in the worst battle in the history of the Marine Corps. My voice is giving out, so I will end here. Thank you for your time."

Suddenly the monument wasn't just a big old piece of metal with a flag sticking out of the top. It came to life before our eyes through the heartfelt words of a son who did indeed have a father who was a hero then . . . and now.

Michael T. Powers

6

TOUGH ROADS, GREAT ACHIEVEMENTS

It is with the heart that one sees rightly; what is essential is invisible to the eye.

Antoine de Saint-Exupéry

Daddy Hands

I submit to you that if a man hasn't discovered something he will die for, he isn't fit to live.

Martin Luther King, Jr.

I awoke in the night to find my husband, Marty, gently rocking our baby son, Noah. I stood for a moment in the doorway, watching this amazing man with whom I was so blessed to share my life lovingly stroke Noah's fat pink cheeks in an effort to comfort him. I felt in my heart that something was seriously wrong with Noah. This was one of several nights Noah had been up, burning with a high fever.

Tears filled my eyes as I watched my beautiful husband move Noah's little cheek up against his own chest so that Noah could feel the vibrations of his voice. Noah is deaf. Learning to comfort him has brought a whole new way of thinking for us. We relied on our voices, a soothing lullaby, audio toys, and music to comfort our other children. But with Noah, we need to use touch, his soft *blankie*, sight, the feel of our voices, and most important, the use of sign language to communicate emotions and a sense of comfort to him.

My husband made the sign for "I love you" with his hand and I saw a tear roll down his cheek as he placed Noah's tiny, weak hand on top of his.

We had taken Noah to the doctor more times than I can remember. It had been a week and a half and Noah's fever remained very high and very dangerous, despite everything the doctor or we had tried. I knew in my soul the way only a mother can know that Noah was in trouble.

I gently touched my husband's shoulder and we looked into each other's eyes with the same fear and knowledge that Noah's wasn't getting any better. I offered to take over for him, but he shook his head, and once again, I was amazed at this wonderful man who is the father of my children. When many fathers would have gladly handed over the parenting duties for some much-needed sleep, my husband stayed stubbornly and resolutely with our child.

When morning finally came, we called the doctor and were told to bring him in again. We already knew that he would probably put Noah in the hospital. So, we made arrangements for the other children, packed bags for all three of us, and tearfully drove to the doctor's office once again. Our hearts filled with dread as we waited in a small room, different from the usual examining room we had become used to. Our doctor finally came in, looked Noah over, and told us the news we expected. Noah had to be admitted to the hospital. Now.

The drive to the hospital in a neighboring town seemed surreal. I couldn't focus on anything, couldn't think, couldn't stop crying. My husband reassured me that he felt in his heart that Noah would be okay. We admitted Noah and were taken to his room right away. It was a tortuous night, filled with horrible tests that made my son's tiny little voice echo though the halls as he screamed over and over.

I felt as if I were shattering from the inside out. My husband never wavered in his faith. He comforted me and Noah and everyone who called to check on Noah. He was a rock.

When the first batch of tests was done, the nurse informed us that a spinal tap would be performed soon. Meningitis was suspected. Marty and I prayed together with Noah. Our hands intertwined, we held our son, and the love of my life lifted his voice to the Lord, telling him how grateful we were for this awesome little spirit with whom he had entrusted us. With tears streaming down his face, he humbly asked the Lord to heal our son. My heart filled with comfort and gratitude.

A short time later, the resident doctor came in. He told us that Noah's first results were back, and that he had *Influenza A.* No spinal tap was needed! Noah would recover and soon be back to his zesty, tornado little self. And Noah was already standing up in the hospital crib, bouncing like he was on a trampoline. My husband's talk with the Lord was already being answered.

Marty and I grinned at each other through our tears, and we waited for Noah to be released from the hospital. Finally, in the middle of the night, our own doctor came in and told us that it was fine to take Noah home. We couldn't pack fast enough!

A few days later, I was cooking dinner. Noah was healing slowly but surely. I felt at peace and knew my husband was the greatest father I could ever want for my children. I peeked around the corner into the living room and chuckled at the picture I saw. There was my husband sitting in his "daddy chair," Noah on his lap. They were reading a book, Dad taking Noah's teeny hands to help him form the signs for the words in the book. They both looked up and caught me watching them, and my husband and I simultaneously signed "I love you" to each other, then to Noah. And then Noah put his little arm up, trying to shape his chubby hand in his own effort to sign "I love you" to his daddy. I watched with tears as my husband carefully helped him form his tiny fingers into the sign with his own gentle hands. Daddy hands.

Susan Farr-Fahncke

Lessons Learned at Little League

Fatherhood, for me, has been less a job than an unstable and surprising combination of adventure, blindman's bluff, guerrilla warfare, and crossword puzzle.

Frederic F. Van de Water

I am standing near the bench at a town Little League field while my ten-year-old son stands at the ready in the batter's box. He sees the bases are filled with his teammates, the score is tied, two outs, the pitcher holds a small white sphere that he is about to fire in his direction, and if things go awry it might smack him the head and hurt a lot.

I am the assistant coach, unwilling to be the manager because my temperament is ill-suited to the tidal waves of pain and joy and sorrow that ten-year-old boys must endure to compete in Little League. In my role, I need never lose my patience or make tough decisions about why Tyler plays right field rather than shortstop. Here, the buck slips past and never stops at me, which is just fine and right and proper.

Mostly I am here because I believe that my presence

will help my ten-year-old play the game better. I believe this because this theory worked extremely well when he was six, seven, eight, even nine, when Little League was a different animal.

Now at this level, the game has become serious. The kids pitch to each other (at lower levels, we coaches would toss cream puffs to our own players so they could smack them and get hits and feel awesomely talented). At this level, an umpire calls balls and very liberal strikes and there is no forgiveness or seven or eight more chances. This is where the wheat starts to get separated from the chaff, and there is no hiding the fact that some of the boys can catch and throw and hit and make the plays and some of the boys can't.

At this level we have umpires and standings and play-offs and the first real whiff of that unmistakable scent called pressure. It is still fun, but fun has become a tiny by-product. It is a taste of real life disguised as a recreational youth activity. And because of this, it is good and visceral and unremittingly tortuous for the species that set up all this: parents.

And so I am at this field, my boy is at the plate, and all I want is for something good to emerge from this moment. My boy is not the big, aggressive, agile, and athletic one. He is the timid, sweet one with the smile of an angel, the heart the size of Jupiter, and the athletic genetics of his mother, whose closest brush with sports was tossing my basketball shoes in the closet back when we were married. But he plays baseball because I immersed him in the beauty and poetry of the game from the moment I could get his little hand to hold a baseball.

He plays because we have spent more hours than I can count in the backyard or the park catching and throwing and hitting and pretending he was the shortstop for the Red Sox and making all the greatest plays in history. He plays because I always believed there was something good about being part of a team and learning how it feels to win and lose and participate. And mostly he plays because he really wants to.

He has refused soccer and football and basketball. But baseball has been his game, a glove tied up with a baseball and soaked with Neatsfoot oil under his bed as a talisman of the season to come.

And perhaps I shouldn't be here anymore because the tension inside me billows to absurd proportions when my son is in the spotlight of the game. The season has gotten off to a horrible start, and our team has yet to win, and my son has yet to actually hit the ball. We have reached a juncture where a groundball of any kind would be victory, where I ache for him to avoid yet another failure. I am well-grounded in the team mentality and know logically that I shouldn't be fixated on his performance. *This is a bunch of ten-year-olds, for crying out loud. Get a grip,* I think to myself.

I wish I could report that the pitcher fired in a smooth one and that my son launched a base hit into left field, driving in two runs. But he stood in, brave as a soldier, and didn't flinch or move his bat as the ball floated tantalizingly and agonizingly straight over the plate.

"Strike three!" the umpire yelled.

And there in that moment, when he turned back to the bench, his face red, and he searched out my eyes, I felt the very rope of the journey that ties him to me, as it tied me to my father, and he to his. I felt the rip of having to hand him this imperfect world, where failure is a rite of passage and so much depends on chances taken on sunny Saturday afternoon diamonds. And I managed, because I am the grown-up, after all, to swallow that giant ache and hand him his glove and send him into right field with a sturdy "We'll get 'em next time, big guy."

Inevitably, he did get that first hit and we won our first

game and we experienced the soaring joy of triumph that makes us want to play these games. But I believe I learned more about us during the struggle. There is, I have come to understand, real joy in Mudville, even after the strike-outs and errors and the games have ended.

The joy is in the steely bond that brings fathers out with sons to don their gloves and toss the ball across green fields of love and devotion. The joy is in being there, together, win or lose, and etched forever in a churning life.

Glenn Rifkin

"Son, you're a chip off the 'ole block."

He's My Son

My husband, Michael, and I were considering adopting again. I had three older children, and Michael and I had adopted two beautiful little girls. This time we were thinking of a son. We searched various online adoption sites and decided it was time to call our caseworker.

"Hi," I said. "We're contemplating adoption again. Would you be able to visit us to update our home study?"

"Sure," she replied. "As a matter of fact, I have a file for a nineteen-month-old special-needs little guy from China. Would you and Michael be interested in seeing it?"

"Man, that's fast, but, yes, we'd be happy to look at it," I answered for both of us.

My husband was at work when the file arrived. I opened it and gazed upon the sweetest little face, a face that I knew belonged to our son. I sobbed as I held his picture to my heart. When Michael came home I was quiet. I didn't want to tell him what I was feeling and influence his decision. I simply handed him the file. He opened it, and when his eyes fell upon the enclosed picture, tears streamed down his face. "This is my son; this is my son," he whispered.

I immediately placed the happy call. "He's the one. Let's go for it."

"Cool! Let's schedule a time to meet and get the ball rolling," the caseworker said. We began the paperwork marathon, which seemed to take forever, but before we knew it, we were in a hotel in China.

We were called to our guide's room and our son, whom we named Mason, was brought to us. He had arthrogryposis. Both hands were balled into fists and hung limply from his wrists. He had little or no bicep muscles, so his arms would not bend at the elbow. His right leg was scissored against his little body, and both feet were clubbed. But our hearts were filled with love as he was placed in our arms.

"Hello, son. We're your mommy and daddy," we said. He didn't cry, but he didn't smile, either.

We took our precious blessing back to our room, bathed him, and decked him out in new clothes. He still didn't smile. We played with him, but he remained unmoved. Crying would have been better than the numbness we thought he was showing. We fed him and changed him into soft, new pajamas. Michael gave Mason his bottle and he fell asleep on his daddy's chest.

Michael sat and held him for a long time. Then he put him into his crib. "I don't think I can do this," he said. "Why isn't he responding to us like Michelle did?" (Our youngest daughter was also adopted from China. When she was placed in our arms, she cried for a solid hour, but after she was bathed, dressed in a new outfit, and we had played with her, she started smiling and talking. Our domestically adopted daughter, Mackenzie, has been with us since her birth. We had never experienced detachment before.)

"Things will be different tomorrow, you'll see," I said. While Michael showered, I knelt by the bed and prayed for my new son and his daddy.

The next morning when Mason realized we were still

there, he smiled. Now he knew we weren't going to leave him. Michael roughhoused and played with him and he laughed and laughed. As I watched the two of them together, I couldn't hold back the tears.

What a pair those two are today! Mason has undergone several surgeries and much therapy. He's walking and running now, and using his hands to feed himself and throw balls to his daddy. He's super smart, loves to give hugs and kisses, and he's a definite chatterbox, too.

Recently, we were hiking a woodland trail and Mason was ahead of us. Michael nodded toward him and whispered to me, "Look, he's my son." Then he said, "You go, champ!" Mason beamed from ear to ear.

Sherry Honeycutt Hatfield

Fathers and Sons and Grandfathers and Angels

The heart has its reasons which reason knows not of.

Blaise Pascal

"Come on, Dad. Let's play!" Ray says the moment his daddy walks in the door.

David laughs and playfully tousles Ray's hair. "Give me a minute. Let me change."

Their daily routine began years ago. When Ray was little, he'd have bats and balls lined up at the edge of the driveway, awaiting his daddy's return from work so he could snag him for play without a moment's delay.

"Do you mind?" David asks, depositing his work clothes in the hamper and then coming back into the kitchen to plant a kiss on my check.

I cup my hand on the stubble of David's face. He winks at me. Our twelve-year-old son stands before us, holding his bat in one hand, a bucket of balls in the other. He is impatient, but only because he is eager for the highlight of his day—time with his daddy. How could I possibly mind?

I laugh. "Go. Have fun. I'll see you two at dinner."

They don their ball caps, climb into the Vette, adjust the music to their liking, and back out of the driveway. They grin, looking like two peas in a pod—the spitting image of each other with their husky builds, strong angular faces, and what David calls "the Sherman nose." They wave as the car rumbles down the road, and I wave back until they turn out of sight. Those two fellows, my favorites in all the world, are best friends.

David knows a life that, God willing, Ray will never know. He knows what it is like to be a boy growing up without a father. His daddy died just before David turned two. We have a handful of photographs, even one or two capturing the image of David and his dad together, but otherwise, David has no recollection, no memories whatsoever of his father. And still, David has gotten fatherhood so right. I know his spirit. I know his heart, and I know some of the men he has loved and who have loved him back. I was honored to have known his grandfather. My mind wanders back to that kind man.

"He was a good man, a kind, gentle man," David says of his daddy's daddy. "He never raised his voice, never uttered a single curse word that I can remember." To this day, David's eyes mist when we walk past a tobacco shop in the mall and the smell reminds him of his grandfather's pipe. When we were first married, David had puffed at a pipe, too. Probably would still if we didn't heed the hazards of smoking.

A year prior to his death, David's grandfather suffered a stroke that left his speech slurred to the point of being barely decipherable, and with a partial paralysis that made living in his two-level home next to impossible. We drove from Texas to Pennsylvania that summer so David might help his grandparents relocate from their home to an assisted living facility. His grandfather hardly spoke, but that did not matter to David. What mattered was being there for this man who meant the world to him, and who was his closest tie to his father. Those few days were the last they were to spend together. Just before we left, I snapped a photograph of Ray, David, and his grandfather on the front steps outside their home. Three generations captured in a photograph, and I had imagined David's father was right there, with them in spirit.

And then came the angels . . .

Two years after his grandfather's death, David experienced a life-threatening illness. Several months before we realized he was so sick and six months before the illness came to a head, David had a premonition. It was just before Christmas.

"Did I talk in my sleep last night?" David asked as we were making the bed one morning.

"Not that I recall," I said. "Why?"

"It's nothing. I was just wondering." He grew quiet and didn't seem to want to talk so I didn't press him further. But a few days later he approached the subject again. "I had a dream."

"Tell me about it," I urged.

"I was with my father and grandfather. They said everything is going to be all right."

"They said that? Did you see them in person? Did you hear your father's voice?"

He tried to explain. "I didn't really see them, but I knew I was with them. They didn't say the words out loud, but that was their message."

I was confused. "What are they talking about? What's going to be all right?"

David shook his head. "I don't know."

Six months later, we understood the meaning of the

dream. David was hospitalized when he could barely breathe. The doctors discovered his body had been throwing blood clots that had shut down two-thirds of his lung capacity and nearly took his life. A dislodged blood clot had taken his father's life . . . I believe with all my heart and soul that the spirits of David's father and grandfather had revealed themselves in David's dream and were looking after him and keeping him safe. I silently thanked them again, as I had so many times before.

A couple of hours later my two fellows arrive home from the ballpark.

"You should've seen the ball I hit, Mom," Ray calls.

"Tell her about that catch you made," David adds.

I hear the details of their exploits and achievements, but what I watch, what my heart listens to, is the interaction between them: the way their eyes light up, the way they smile at each other, and the friendly jabs and back-and-forth banter. I see the love they share and how they enjoy their time together. I see in our son's eyes his adoration of his father, and in my husband's eyes, his devotion to our son.

Ray's baseball coach recently told the boys, "Life isn't always fair, but we play the hand we're dealt." David has lived this motto every single day I've known him. Certainly, our son loves his father, but I believe this love will only grow deeper and stronger as he grows older and wiser. And I know without a doubt that someday, if and when he has children of his own, he will be just as awesome a father to them as his father is to him. Life is blessed.

Tracey L. Sherman

Rite of Passage

Anyone who has never made a mistake has never tried anything new.

Albert Einstein

A gray dawn broke over the leaden waters of Lake Eugenia, heralding the final day of my fishing trip with my son. So far it had been a disaster. Everything had gone wrong. We had snagged our propeller, tangled tackle, lost lures, and punctured a hole in our inflatable boat. Worst of all, we had not caught a single fish!

Our misadventures began after my nine-year-old, Rob, talked me into taking him on his first fishing trip. Now, you must understand that I have a decidedly limited enthusiasm for outdoor activity. Walks on nature trails and fishing off the dock at a friend's cottage highlight my wilderness experience. Rob, however, was determined to have an outdoor adventure with Dad.

When we arrived at the lake, we noted the partially submerged stumps and lily pads dotting the surface of the bay. The conditions were ideal! We could almost see the fish flicking their fins, daring us to catch them!

We eagerly emptied the truck and made camp. Then after inflating our boat, we mounted the motor, loaded our fishing tackle, and launched. However, our quest for fish got off to a slow start. Initially, much of our time was spent dodging stumps and constantly cleaning our propeller of weeds. Then after we had barely wetted our lines, the wind rose, the waves crested, our small electric motor began to labor, and we started to drift! We forgot about fishing, and in desperation unshipped the oars. With Rob rowing and me coaxing the motor, we fought our way safely back to shore. I was certain I heard the fish giggling.

Well, no matter! Dining in the "great outdoors" would lift our spirits! We began to prepare our first camp-cooked meal: steak and home fries, seared over an open fire. The wind blew, the flames flickered, smoke swirled, and our eyes watered. But regardless of singed eyebrows and sec-ond-degree burns to our hands, we persevered! And despite the fact that our steaks were charred on the out-side, raw on the inside, and seasoned with first-aid oint-ment, we dined with relish. We topped off our meal by toasting some marshmallows, then retreated to the tent to sleep. I dozed off to the sound of waves lapping gently against the shore. Apparently Rob didn't. He maintains that my snoring not only drowned out the music of the night, but also would probably have deterred a rabid wolf.

Awaking refreshed, at 5:30 AM, we shivered over card-board boxes of snack-pack cereal and sallied forth at first light. The fish, however, decided to sleep in. By noon we had had enough and limped back to the dock with a still empty stringer and literally, "that sinking feeling." Not only were our egos deflating, but so was our boat! A sub-merged stump had holed the largest floatation chamber in our rubber raft, and we were losing air at an alarming rate. Undaunted, we dug out the patching kit and carried out running repairs. We could cope!

And then, the rains came!

Donning sou'westers and looking like Atlantic fishermen in a toy boat, we struck out again. Damp but determined, we stuck with it, stalking our finned quarry around the lake, trying every lure in our tackle boxes, and testing each technique; all in vain. The sun came out, but the fish didn't, and our lures remained untouched.

Eventually time ran out, and as the sun began to set, I was forced to turn the boat for home. Rob sat facing me, his shoulders slumped in disappointment and trolling his bait behind while we concocted elaborate excuses to explain our lack of success. We were fishing failures!

As our bow approached the dock, I shut down the motor and Rob reluctantly began to retrieve his lure. Suddenly, the line jerked taut and streaked away from the boat. He pulled back and a huge large-mouth bass exploded from the lake. The fight was on!

Rob's rod bowed as fins and fingers strained in combat. His wily opponent leaped, twisted, turned, and dove, using every trick it knew in its fight for freedom. But the hook held and Rob slowly gained ground. Then catastrophe struck. In the midst of this titanic struggle, our temporary patch popped loose and air began to hiss angrily from our rubber raft. We were sinking!

I sprang into action! Alternating between pumping, panting, and shouting enthusiastic, if not expert, instructions, I did my best to keep us afloat. But it was a losing battle. We were going down fast!

As our boat sank slowly to the bottom, that mighty fish broke water time and again, dancing on its tail, trying valiantly to throw the hook. The struggle continued, and my heart pounded in my throat as father and son stood side by side, knee deep in water in our sunken craft, working together to land that battling bass. Then the line went limp!

Time stood still as Rob reeled furiously, taking up the slack. Was our quarry still hooked? That question was answered in an instant by another great leap. Scales of green and gold glistened in the spray as that bass burst from the water and splashed down right beside us. I scooped and with a cry of triumph netted our catch.

Shaking with excitement, we abandoned ship and waded to shore, bearing our prize on high. During the struggle some fellow campers had gathered near the dock and their cries of "Way to go, kid!" and "Great fish!" filled our ears! My chest swelled with pride as Rob lifted that "lunker" from the net and strained to hold it aloft. Cameras clicked. We noted the measurements. Then Rob gently placed that monarch of the lake in the dockside holding tank.

That night we sat at our campfire, reliving the battle. Instant celebrities and now seasoned veterans, we dispensed sage angling advice to any and all who stopped by to see "the fish."

Morning came. We loaded the truck. It was time to go, but we knew we had one thing left to do. Rob walked alone out onto the dock, paused for a moment, and then carefully tipped the tank, spilling the water and returning his fish to its watery lair. A magical moment, a rite of passage, and a special memory in the lives of both father and son. We would share many more.

John Forrest

Visiting Dad

As we try to change, we will discover within us a fierce struggle between our loyalty to that battle-scarred victim of his own childhood, our father, and the father we want to be.

Augustus Y. Napier

Hi, Dad! I'm back. I hope you recognize me with my gray hair. It's been awhile. I'm wearing my travel clothes because I'm here in Detroit on business. I retired from classroom teaching, but I'm doing consulting work now. Dad, I've always been grateful to you for telling me I needed an education to get ahead in this world. You were so right.

In Proverbs 15:5, it says: "Only a fool despises his father's advice; a wise son considers each suggestion" (TLB).

Because I followed your advice, I had a good thirty-year career and I thank you, but today I thought I'd bring you up-to-date on family matters and just, you know, say hello.

Have any of the other kids been here to talk with you? We're all fine, Dad, except for June. All of her children were grown before she left. She should be with you now. She always said she knew she'd get cancer, "Just like Daddy did." From her experience, I have taught my children "Be careful what you ask for. You might get it."

Six of us grew up without you, Dad. After you died, we had to learn on our own what we could and could not do. In junior high Gary and I learned we were pretty good fighters. Then we had football in high school, which relieved some aggressions for us.

Gary ran track in the spring. I played baseball. Joey played all sports and he was very good. Several colleges were after him, but sports didn't bring him much satisfaction. Something in his life was missing—an admiring father. You were never in the stands cheering for him. He was only four years old when you died, and he never did learn to pretend he didn't miss you, not the way the rest of us did.

When was the last time I visited your grave? I think it was the time I came out here, stood on the grass, and hollered at you for dying and leaving Mom and us kids. I'm sorry about the hollering. I know you didn't ask to leave. You had no choice, Dad, but I was having marital problems at the time, and you weren't around to support me. Children are very judgmental of their parents, aren't they? And parents are easy to blame for things, especially when they are no longer around.

Actually, you were never around. I always resented your being at some bar drinking and singing with your friends. I hated the smell of those places every time Mom sent me in to get you. She broke your guitar once, but that didn't keep you home. Gary has a drinking problem today, you know, and Joey does drugs, but we can't talk to them about their addictions any more than anyone could have told you about yours.

Whew! Sorry about the outburst, Dad. What's weird is

that rage happens only when I have these talks with you. I've asked God to help me bear that load, and He does help . . . everywhere but here.

When you were bedridden, just before my twelfth birthday, our lives changed drastically. Your illness altered our routines, drained our energies, and added tension to our day-to-day chores. Your stomach cancer became our lives.

I prayed for you. I lit candles for you. I watched you drink that little vial of water sent from Lourdes, France, and I expected a healing, but nothing happened. Someone had a plan for you that was different from my own.

I wish our visits weren't so short. I would like to sit down and talk with you, but there's no bench to sit on. There's just grass. You said to not waste any money on a grave marker because you wouldn't be here anyway. You'd be in heaven. Maybe your children can chip in for a marker. Your final resting place will then be easy to find.

If we had more time together, I would tell you about Anne and Mary and what great people your daughters have become. All that love they missed giving you, they stored up and then poured all over their children and grandchildren. It's beautiful to see.

Mary has become a wonderful poet. Anne hugs everybody, Dad. She would train you to hug, if you didn't already know how. Men of your generation didn't hug, did they?

What would it be like to meet you today? I often wonder about that. Would you hug me, Dad, or would we shake hands?

How different would my life be had you lived? Would you have kept me in school in Michigan? Would you have allowed me to join the Navy, to become a teacher, to have married when I did? One thing we could not do is have a drink together. I'm a teetotaler.

You have been gone since 1948, but to tell the truth, Dad, I never got used to your being gone. Does anyone ever get used to losing a loved one?

The grass under my shoes is soft, and I sense that your spirit is nearby. This humid Michigan air is cooling off, and as I think of a special time I had with you, Dad, I can feel myself relaxing . . .

Your black 1941 Hudson, a big bubble of a car, brought us home from school that day. You were healthy then, so I must have been ten years old. You told me to sweep the basement floor before I went out to play, although sweeping was not part of our daily routine. You also had a strange smile on your face.

I argued for sweeping the floor later. You insisted. I pounded down the wooden steps, grumbling, questioning parents, and hating that dumb old basement.

Then I caught my breath. Time stood still. At the bottom of the steps, with bright golden sunlight streaming in through the narrow basement windows, I saw it. I think I heard a choir of angels singing. The sun shone directly onto the most beautiful red bicycle in the whole history of civilization! You had brought it home from Sears for me.

An outpouring of love always follows that memory, Dad. And that's the case today, over fifty years later.

By the way, I forgot to sweep out the basement. Sorry.

Hard feelings have now been replaced with soft ones.

We got a lot accomplished today, but I think I'll work toward getting a marker put on your grave before my next visit. A father should be easy to find.

I have a lot more to discuss with you—my first game at Briggs Stadium, fishing off the dock in Lake St. Claire, and our trip in the Hudson back to your hometown in Kansas.

Dad, I didn't know I could remember so many good times with you until I tried!

Let's end this visit with the same ritual we went

through to end our days when you were alive and had us pray together in the living room. Just let me put my handkerchief on the grass so that when I kneel down I won't soil my pants. Okay.

If you will be my prayer partner, we can begin: "Our Father, who art in heaven . . ."

John J. Lesjack

Jason's Story

Jason always seemed to need extra time with his school-work. He came to my attention when he entered my fifth-grade class. He did not seem focused and would often look out the window. When he took a test, he would be only halfway finished when time ran out. His mother was concerned and hoped that he would grow out of it. He made it through the year and was now in my sixth-grade home-room class and continued to have a difficult time with his work. Jason required a lot of patience, and with so many students, patience was not always available.

I gave my students a project: they were to write their own books. The Nationwide book company gave a book kit for each student. The company would bind each manu-script with a hardcover, making it look like a real library book. Students took the task to heart and created little masterpieces. Each book needed eight pages of text with some pages having illustrations. They could use photos, but they had to be scanned. I allotted them six weeks to finish. Proofreading created a lot of extra work for me.

I set a date to read first drafts and another date when the finished manuscripts had to be packed up and sent to the printer. Jason told me he had a hard time thinking of anything to write. Some students were writing about fantastic space battles in make-believe worlds, and others were writing about their favorite vacations to distant lands. I began asking Jason, on a daily basis, to see his first draft, and the answer was always the same. He couldn't think of anything to write. I told him to write something that was personal, something he knew about. He looked more confused than ever, and I had run out of patience.

Finally, on the day before the manuscripts were to be shipped out, Jason came up to my desk, holding a stack of crumpled pages—his first draft. I was horrified at the thought of reading it, making corrections, and then getting him to complete it. When I saw that he had glued pictures to the paper and had not scanned them, I took the pages from him and told him it was too late. I scolded him for being so late and sent him back to his seat. With a deep sigh I picked up the pages and thought that checking his story was impossible. No way could I find the time to help him. I dreaded looking through it but glanced at the cover. On it was the title, "The Little Boy Who Lost His Father." Included was a drawing of a butterfly with a sad frown on its face and a cloud with tears falling to the ground. I stared at it and began to feel a pain in my soul. On the next page he had written "Based on a true story."

I looked up and saw Jason seated at his desk, looking out the window. As I read it, I did not notice the misspelled words, the incorrect grammar, or the glue oozing from the edge of the pictures. The pictures were of Jason as a baby and one with his father holding him in his arms. Another showed Jason in his mother's arms, crying and looking at a birthday cake.

He began: "One day a little boy woke up and felt something was wrong. He heard silence in the whole house. He did not understand. His mother was in tears and then he noticed that the one true person who ever meant anything to him was not there. He asked his mommy where was his daddy. She replied, 'Son, he is in a better place.' "

It continued with stories of scary dreams and waking up in the middle of the night screaming out "Daddy!" His mother told him to recite Philippians 4:13: "I can do all things through Him who strengthens me" (NKJV). Repeating this verse over and over, he was finally able to sleep. He wrote about asking God to allow him to speak to his father, if only for one minute, so he could say things he never got a chance to say before he died, to give a hug good-bye. On his fifth birthday he was so sad that he refused to accept any gifts and would not blow out the candles on his cake or even eat it. Nothing else was on his mind but getting that last chance to be with his father. When he turned eight years old, things began to change, and he started to get used to the feelings of emptiness. He felt that he would always have a hole in his heart, but he tried to make peace with himself. When he looked at his mother, he saw her pain, especially when he misbehaved or didn't do well in school.

On the last page Jason wrote, "Finally, as the boy grew up and became mature, he knew what to do when someone you love is gone. He knew that one day he and his father would be together again. He also knew that his father watched over him every day and would never leave his side. So the boy never actually lost his father. They were only separated for a little while."

After regaining my composure, I called Jason. He told me he had written a personal story and had not even told his mother about it. I helped him correct his spelling and grammar, and I scanned his pictures. He had only seven pages of text; he needed to write one more, so I suggested he write a letter to his father.

Dear Father, I wish I could see you for one last time. What have you been doing? I want to ask you so many questions. I am a big boy now, and I am in the sixth grade. I play sports like basketball and football. Mom is doing great so far, and I am being the man of the house and taking care of her. I can't wait to see you again one day. Your son, Jason. PS I love you!

Few dry eyes remained when anyone read Jason's book. His mother told me that she did not know he had written the story, and it had caused a profound impact at home. Her husband's relatives had thought Jason had forgotten his father, but when they read the book, it succeeded in bringing the family closer. The book got the attention of a local TV station, and they asked Jason to read parts of his book on the air for Father's Day. While his mother and I spoke about how the book had evolved, I noticed the crew had taken him into their hearts. I saw a confidence and joy in Jason that I had not seen before.

Jason has moved on, and although he continues to struggle with his schoolwork, he has improved. And from time to time he still looks out the window.

Carl Ballenas
As previously appeared in
The Boy Who Lost His Father
by Nationwide Learning

A Grain of Sand

All God's angels come to us disguised.

James Russell Lowell

It was another cold day in Michigan, and the last thing I wanted to do was go outside and do anything. The e-mail on my computer was doing its best to keep my mind busy and help me stay warm; it even provided a smile every now and then.

The serenity of the moment was short-lived and quickly broken by the ringing of the phone on the desk beside me. As I picked up the phone, I noticed the caller ID. It read UNAVAILABLE. I knew this was a good chance it was my younger brother Fred calling on his cell phone.

For the first time in my life, I hoped it wasn't my brother. It wasn't his voice I feared; rather it was the message it might carry, a message concerning the condition of our father. So far the messages hadn't promised much hope for his recovery.

It had been only two weeks since I had left my brother in the 80 degree, sunny weather of Florida. I had to make my way back home to my family and to my job. Fred had taken time away from his business to try to help. The job Fred stayed to do was one of the most important of his life. He stayed to try to help heal our father and, equally important, to be there for our mom, and help to ensure that Dad received the best care they could give him while he was in the hospital.

The doctors kept telling us Dad's chances for recovery weren't very high, and only two weeks earlier his kidneys had begun to shut down, fluid filled one lung, and the other had collapsed.

Our father never gave in, nor did his family. My brother tirelessly led the charge, getting up to the hospital every day at 6 AM to meet with the doctors, spending most of the day there with Dad and Mom, then returning at night to be with Dad as visiting hours ended.

I answered the phone, saying, "Hey, Fred!" I received no answer, and asked, "Fred, is that you?" With a deep breath, he replied a simple, "Yeah—it's me."

Oh, dear God! I said to myself. I waited a moment before asking, "Is Dad all right? Fred, is Dad all right?"

"Yeah, Bill." He took another deep breath. "Dad's all right!"

"Are you all right?" I asked.

"I am okay," he said.

As Fred regained his composure, he said, "You're not going to believe this." And Fred went on to tell a story that explained his deep breathing. . . . But it was a story I did believe!

A few weeks prior to this, Dad couldn't even sit up on his own. He was on the verge of death. But today it was different.

"When I got to Dad's room, there he was, sitting on the edge of his hospital bed, swinging his feet and acting like a happy little kid. Bill, I am not kidding! Dad was giggling like a little boy who was just given a new puppy!"

"Why?" I asked, somewhat confused.

"Dad told me he said he saw God today. God came into his room and told him he was going to be all right! Dad was in his room, and a nurse was checking his signs, when all of a sudden there was a bright light. He saw the light coming down the hall, then it came into his room. The light filled the room. Dad said it made him feel peace, like nothing he had ever felt. God spoke to Dad, telling him he would get better."

"Can I talk to him?"

Dad got on the phone. "Hi, Bill!"

"Wow, Dad, you sound great!" I said. "Tell me what happened today."

He repeated the story about the light, but added a bit to the account about a lady who had come into his room. She took him by the hand and led him out of his room to another place. Dad said, "I think we went down into the basement, but I am not sure. When we got to the room, God was there and the beauty of his light filled the room. There was every color of the rainbow and some colors I have never seen. God never spoke in voice," he explained, "but I could hear every word in his thoughts."

Dad said that God picked up a grain of sand and showed it to him, telling how each grain of sand was a moment of his life; every action, every event he had done in his life was another grain of sand, and each grain led to the next grain. God told of both the good and the bad things of his life, not leaving out one detail. When God finished reviewing my father's life, God asked Dad to look down, showing him that he was standing on a pile of sand. God explained how each action had led him to where he was right now. God told my father he had done all he needed to do in life and then told him he would get better!

Dad said the next thing he knew, the lady who had taken him to the room again took his hand and led him back up to his hospital room. He said, "I could tell she was very beautiful, but I couldn't see her face."

As the lady was about to leave him, she turned toward him for a moment, and in that moment he saw more beauty in her face than he had ever seen in his life.

"Dad, do you think she was an angel?" I asked.

"I didn't see any wings, but I can tell you, her face carried all the beauty of the world, and her eyes reflected all the beauty of heaven.

"Bill, my whole life I have believed in God, but not seeing, I sometimes have doubts. But after today, if God calls me home tomorrow it will be fine. I am not afraid. I know he is always with me and has a plan."

The day my father talked to God was a turning point on his trip back home to all of us. Two weeks later he was given an eightieth-birthday party by his many doctors and nurses. A few weeks after that, he came home again; home to add a few more grains of sand to the many sand castles of our lives.

William Garvey

7

A DAY IN THE LIFE

My father didn't tell me how to live, he lived and let me watch him do it.

Clarence B. Kelland

I Became My Dad Today

I became my dad today
when my son looked at me that way.
That smile upon his face—
there could be no mistake.
When he looked at me that way
I became my dad today.

I became my dad today
when he held my hand that way.
The feeling of the touch
just reminded me so much.
When my son held my hand that way
I became my dad today.

I became my dad today
when I sang to my son that way.
The voice I had heard before
as a child sitting on the floor.

When I sang to him that way
I became my dad today.

Tom Krause

Tuxedo Swimming

This past week I took my three-year-old, Caleb, to his first swimming lesson at the local YMCA. I had been looking forward to some father-son bonding time ever since earlier this year my wife suggested doing this. The day before the first class, I asked Kristi to call the YMCA to find out what we were supposed to bring, what time we were to be there, and any other important details. I work third shift and have a hard time making calls during the day when I'm sleeping, so I just wanted to make sure I knew what I was getting into.

We left half an hour early, just to make sure we were there on time, and went into the locker room to change. We got our swimsuits on, put the rest of our clothes in a gym bag, and proceeded to make our way out through the showers and into the pool area. I was really looking forward to this. Me, my boy, nothing on but our swimsuits, and a pool full of water. What could be better?

I rounded the corner, holding hands with my excited son, and an inaudible gasp of horror escaped me. There in the hall next to the pool were ten to fifteen parents and their young children. All the children had their swimsuits on, but every one of the parents was fully dressed. Let me rephrase that . . . all the mothers were fully dressed. Not another father was to be seen for miles. *I was the only guy!* Some mothers were in dresses and power suits, as if they had just come from the office, while others wore jeans and shirts. But the important thing was *they were all fully dressed!*

I could just hear what they were thinking:

"Who is the three-year-old with the hair on his chest?"

"Can a man really have a chest that goes into his body instead of out?"

"I thought you had to be a corpse to have skin that white."

"My sunglasses! Where are my sunglasses? *Oh, the humanity!*"

"He must have tapeworms. Something has to be stealing his nourishment."

"All this weight equipment at the YMCA and he still looks like that!"

I wanted to scream back at them, "I tried lifting weights, but they're too heavy!"

I wanted to crawl into a hole and hide, but I had nowhere to go.

The nice young high school girls who were teaching the swim class started explaining that the parents were to stay out in the hall and watch their kids through the large windows. The only time they were to go near the pool was if their children were crying or misbehaving. Otherwise the teachers didn't want the children distracted by their parents while learning water safety.

I slowly reached into my gym bag and pulled out my T-shirt. Trying my best to be cool and nonchalant, I covered the top half of my body, and by the time the instructor was done talking, I was fully clothed.

Caleb had a great time as I watched through the

windows and tried to avoid any possible conversation with another human being.

When I came home, the first thing out of Kristi's mouth was "How come you're not wet?"

After I explained what had transpired, she laughed and laughed until her stomach hurt. For some reason, even after the phone call, we were both under the impression that I would get to frolic in the water, too. The best part of the whole story is I have to go back and face these people again today at 4:30 and twice a week for the next month or so.

I think I might rent a tux for today's swimming lesson.

Michael T. Powers

Squirrel Wars

Men are born to succeed, not fail.

Henry David Thoreau

Unaware of the looming danger, oblivious to the war being waged, the new backyard birdfeeder sat majestically on its new pole. Guardrails, metal plates, and inverted saucerlike barriers were guaranteed to prevent all pests, especially squirrels, from pilfering the precious birdfeed. And the pole itself was lubed with so much grease even Spiderman couldn't get a grip.

We sat in the sunroom and congratulated Dad on his latest accomplishment, his latest anti-squirrel contraption. Surrounded by nine family members spanning three generations, Dad beamed with pride. As one, children and grandchildren *oohed* and *aahed* over a steady procession of marvelous mountain birds visiting the new feeder.

When the first squirrel approached, we all crossed our fingers and held our breath. Except Mom. She'd ridden this train before and knew where it was headed. Comfortable in her favorite corner chair, Mom lost herself in her sewing.

Outside the squirrel sized up the situation in all of six seconds, then scurried to the back edge of the backyard. Hope rose in our hearts. Was he giving up?

Mom refused to look.

We knew how clever squirrels could be. We knew they were smart. But we didn't expect this. Like an Olympic pole-vaulter, the squirrel got a running start, picked up speed, blazed across a large decorative boulder, and jumped toward a nearby Japanese maple. He landed on a branch just the right size to hold his weight while bending slightly. Then, like a diving board, the supple branch launched the squirrel high into the air, over the guardrails, over the metal plates, over the inverted saucerlike barriers, and directly to the top of the birdfeeder. He then flipped over, gripped the underside of the top ledge of the feeder, hung upside down and began eating.

Mom just kept sewing.

Dad's decades-old battle to keep squirrels out of his birdfeeders has become something of a legend in our family. It began over thirty years ago when we moved to a big house on a small hill in the Blue Ridge Mountains of western North Carolina. The house was (and is) surrounded by tall trees—including pine, oak, poplar, and hickory—as well as azalea, laurel, rhododendron, and other mountain shrubs. To our great delight, we discovered this lush vegetation harbored an incredible variety of beautiful birds. Not a place one would expect to go to war, but then, war sometimes comes unexpectedly.

The first battle began on an innocent spring day when Dad decided to hang a new birdfeeder from the lowest branch of the big oak not far from the back porch. We soon learned the Blue Ridge Mountains also harbor an incredible number of squirrels. Intelligent squirrels. Unscrupulous little buggers who will gladly steal a meal from a feeder rather than forage for one of their own.

I still remember Dad standing on the back porch, hands on his hips, staring in disbelief as a half-dozen squirrels gorged themselves on fresh birdseed. Legend has it one of the squirrels glanced at Dad and winked. Dad's look of disbelief slowly transformed to anger, coupled with an air of quiet determination. I knew that look. And I knew the squirrels were in trouble.

Dad never took a gun to a squirrel. He was determined to outwit the critters without hurting them. Not an easy task.

If Dad was the general in command of Operation Squirrel, Mom was the chief of staff, watching from a distance and waiting for the right moment to pull the plug and bring the troops home. As eldest son, I served as attaché to the general and liaison to the chief of staff.

Like dressing a child to play in the snow on a frosty winter day, we created layer after layer of birdfeeder protection in a vain attempt to confuse the clever squirrels. First, Dad removed the feeder from the oak branch and hung it from a clothesline strung between two trees. This did not prove much of a challenge for the acrobatic little rodents. With a twinkle in their eyes and snickers on their faces, the smug squirrels easily negotiated the clothesline.

Next, Dad took some old 33-1/3 LPs (vinyl record albums, for those old enough to remember; probably the Dean Martin albums Mom never liked) and strung them on the clothesline on either side of the birdfeeder. The agile squirrels simply jumped the records, landed nimbly on the line, and continued on to the feeder.

For another layer of protection, I helped Dad cut the bottoms off of some plastic, two-liter soft drink bottles (newfangled inventions at the time). We strung the bottomless bottles on the clothesline between the records. Then we joined with the younger recruits (my three siblings) and the chief of staff on the back porch. We all watched in wonder as squirrel after squirrel climbed a tree, walked the clothesline, jumped an album, scurried across a two-liter bottle, jumped another album, and so on until finally finding their reward in a meal of succulent birdseed.

Discouraged but undaunted, the general and I hurried to the hardware store and returned with a tube of grease the size of Fort Dix. We put a thick layer of brown grease on everything: the clothesline, the records, the two-liter bottles. This final layer of protection proved a challenge, but not a defeat, to the amazing squirrels. Some fell to the ground trying to negotiate the greased soft-drink bottles, but quickly got up and tried again. In the end, the squirrels were slowed, but not stopped, as they continued raiding the birdfeeder.

Meanwhile, the anti-squirrel devices had become a hideous eyesore in our otherwise beautiful backyard. No longer amused, Mom began to wonder, "What was the point of attracting pretty birds to a yard containing such an unsightly mess?" Since his contraptions weren't working anyway, Dad reluctantly took them down and admitted defeat . . . for a time.

Over the next three decades, Dad experimented with a variety of birdfeeders and anti-squirrel devices. Some were store-bought. Some were homemade. None were completely effective. Until recently.

Dad sometimes complained, "If we can put a man on the moon, why can't we keep squirrels out of birdfeeders?" Eventually, modern technology did just that, with a new, motorized birdfeeder. This little gem contains a round platform on which a bird can sit while feeding, but the weight of a squirrel will activate a motor, turn the platform, and spin the squirrel to the ground.

Victory at last!

And yet, victory is not always what you think. On a

recent trip home for New Year's Day, I was surprised to find Dad sliding open the sunroom door and tossing peanuts to the squirrels.

"What's up with this?" I asked.

Dad got a sheepish look on his face. "Keeps the squirrels out of the feeders."

I nodded skeptically. "Uh-huh. And?"

He shrugged. "And it's winter. It's twenty degrees out. Squirrels have to eat, too."

I laughed. "Gone soft in your old age, have you, general?"

He ignored me and threw another handful of peanuts toward a pair of squirrels. I glanced at Mom. She just smiled and continued with her needlepoint.

Over the next twenty minutes, Dad and I ate half a bag of peanuts and fed the other half to squirrels, chipmunks, and other hard-luck cases. I couldn't believe I was actually feeding the squirrels. And yet as I thought about it, I realized that's the warrior's way. Once an enemy is defeated, you treat him with compassion and respect.

The general is now retired. He still enjoys an occasional skirmish with the squirrels, but for the most part, the truce remains intact. Still, I have moments when I can't help but long for the days of old, when the squirrels were undefeated, soft drinks were sold in glass bottles, and music was still played on 33-1/3 LPs.

Carl Dennison

The Birthday Party

"Moms! Bring your child to Aaron's Fifth Birthday Party at Romp 'n' Roam this Saturday at noon! There will be pizza and cake for the kids and plenty of fun for everyone!"

"See?" I told my wife, holding out the invitation decorated with bright blue racing cars so she could read it. "This clearly says 'moms.' Not 'dads.' 'Moms.' I'm not invited."

Raising her head weakly from her pillow, my wife squinted at the invitation. "Jane just put down 'moms' because we're usually the ones who bring the kids to parties. But she won't mind if you take Joe. I called her and told her that I have the flu. She says it will be nice to have a dad at Romp 'n' Roam for a change."

Nice? I had my doubts about that. Romp 'n' Roam is a huge indoor playground in our town, filled with tunnels, slides, and colorful plastic balls kids love to jump into. I'd visited Romp 'n' Roam before but always with my wife at my side so that she could follow the kids around while I drank coffee and read the newspaper. "Does Joe mind if I take him?" I asked, looking for another way out of Daddy Duty.

"Why would Joe mind?"

"Well, he's used to going places with you. Maybe it would upset him if I took him to the party."

Shutting her eyes, my wife rolled onto her side. "It's just a birthday party for a five-year-old," she reminded me. "I'm not missing his high school graduation or his wedding. Besides, it's about time you took him somewhere alone."

She had a point. In the five years since Joe's birth, my wife had been his chief caregiver, a role she delighted in. And to be completely honest, that was just fine with me. While I loved my son from the moment I first saw him, he also mystified me with his variety of cries and demands that I couldn't interpret, but which my wife was able to immediately identify as pleas for a clean diaper, food, or a nap. He also wiggled so much that I was almost afraid to hold him—suppose he leaped out of my arms like a puppy or squirmed his way through my hands like a freshly caught fish? Not that I didn't do many things with him: cuddling, playing, reading at bedtime, even changing diapers. But social life? That I hadn't yet tackled. Later, I told myself as the years passed, when Joe's older I'll do more things with him. Father and son things, like working on the car and shoveling the driveway.

Not like taking him to a birthday party at Romp 'n' Roam, however. That particular activity was never one I would have picked out on my own.

The day of Aaron's birthday party was bright and cold. Joe and I arrived at Romp 'n' Roam precisely at noon, and we were greeted by Jane and what seemed like ten thousand moms, all talking about things like the best place to get highlights for their hair, their favorite recipes for pasta, and breastfeeding. A wave of shyness swept over me. As novel as the idea was to be the only man in all that female company, it was more than a touch daunting.

Joe tugged on my hand. "Want to play with me, Dad?" he asked. Like a chip off the old block, he seemed to be having an attack of timidity, too.

"All right," I readily agreed, "what shall we do?"

"Follow me," Joe suggested.

And so I did. Up ladders and down slides. Through tunnels and mazes. Into pits filled with balls, where Joe and I happily pelted each other. This is fun, I realized as I crawled after my son, ignoring my aching knees and occasional feelings of claustrophobia. A lot more fun than I'd thought it would be.

The party ended with the promised pizza and cake for the kids and coffee for the grown-ups. "It's wonderful to see a dad playing with his son," one of the moms remarked to me. "I can tell that the two of you have a good time together."

Smiling down at my son, I agreed. "He's just about the best company I know," I told her, happy that I'd learned I didn't need to wait until my son was old enough to hold a screwdriver or shovel to spend some quality time with him. Quality time is where you find it, even at an indoor playground in the middle of winter.

Mark Musolf

Stroller Derby Season

You can discover more about a person in an hour of play than in a year of conversation.

Plato

Stroller derby season is in full bloom again. It happens like clockwork every spring. As soon as the snow melts, the stroller invasion begins. They crowd the sidewalks, jockeying for position. Every year, of course, a few new entrants join the field—and a few have called it quits.

I don't know what the rule of thumb is for when a kid is considered too old for a stroller. But I had not-so-secretly wished that this was the year for my kid. Over the long winter, we even put one of our two strollers out to pasture. But we held on to one just in case we ever needed it. That same Principle of Junk explains why we have barely enough room for our one car in our two-car garage.

The reality is that my son, who is now pushing four, had been pushing away the stroller for some time. The old jalopies are growing cobwebs just sitting there in the garage taking up precious space.

That is until a light pole sideswiped the vehicle I drive

(and, no, Officer Friendly, it was not the other way around), causing a chain-reaction series of events that ended with yours truly pushing an empty stroller to my son's day care one fine spring day.

As I pushed nearer the day care, I heard the kids. When I heard my son's name, I looked up to the second-floor where I saw a bunch of his classmates sticking their heads out the window. Unlike me, they thought it was cool that I was pushing a stroller instead of driving a car. That apparently rubbed off on my son, who, rather surprisingly, showed great glee at being chauffeured home in his Model T stroller.

A bit of a hill is on the route home, and I asked if he wanted to go faster. A smile broke across his face as he nodded. *Gentlemen, push your strollers*, I heard in my head. There we were racing down the hill, passing all the newer deluxe models, and he sat up partway in his seat and shook his fist in the air like a jockey going for the roses.

At the bottom of the hill, he urged, "More!" to a winded and rusty Daddy.

"After we cross," I told him, needing to replenish my fuel supply.

The sidewalk in front of our house was wide with lots of room to maneuver, so I knew it would be a good one for us to let loose on. When we reached it, I half-jokingly asked, "Should we just take it easy and go nice and slow?"

Speed Racer's head zipped around. "No, go fast!"

"You sure?"

"Uh-huh," he said, grinning from ear to ear.

Down the block we zoomed, Daddy huffing and puffing, and Speed Racer's giggling and fist-waving serving as the whip. It was one of those most unexpected father-son moments, when your kid brings out the kid in you that rarely gets out—especially on a public thoroughfare.

The problem was that daddies, unlike their sons, lack an

endless supply of fuel. When this daddy finally pushed the stroller into its spot in the garage, his tank was on empty.

Several days and several more stroller rides later, my vehicle was back in its proper place in the garage, its battered side mended so that you couldn't even tell it had been bruised. That day I happily buckled myself into the driver's seat and set off to pick up my boy.

As we walked out the door of the day care, my son turned to where the stroller should have been. "No stroller today?"

"No, remember, we got the car back. It's right over there." I pointed.

My son sulked in his car seat.

"You like the stroller better?" I asked, already reading the answer on my son's face.

The next day I was back to pushing the stroller. Only now, I noticed the stares from passersby as I pushed an empty stroller. In the days that followed, I saw this reaction more and more. Even a little girl in a passing stroller pointed out the obvious. It was as if she was saying, "Um, sir, you forgot something."

I nodded and pushed on. Soon, I knew, the solid green flag would be waved and that the little driver at the controls would push me to my limit with that call, "Go fast!"

Randy Richardson

Lightning Bugs and Fireworks

On the Fourth of July, Kristi and I went a couple blocks from our house to a huge hill where we could enjoy the view and the fireworks not only from the town we live in, but also from nearby towns. It was a hot night, but a wonderful breeze gave occasional relief, and we could see a long way in all directions.

I wanted to see the reaction of Caleb, our three-year-old, to the fireworks. He sat with us all of two minutes before he started giggling and tumbling down the hill.

"Caleb, come here."

He reluctantly came back by us and sat for a spell.

"See the pretty colors over there?"

"Ooohhh!" he replied, all the while looking in a different direction from where the fireworks were actually going off.

"Heee-heee!" he giggled as he tumbled down the steep hill again.

"Caleb, come here and watch with Daddy."

"Okay, Daddy."

Back up the hill he came. I tried to get him to concentrate on the fireworks again.

He watched for another twenty seconds before he started walking away from us.

He let out a sudden squeal of delight. *Finally, he is enjoying the fireworks,* I thought.

"Look at all the lightning bugs!" he yelled out.

I sighed and looked down the hill; indeed, literally hundreds of fireflies were stealing Daddy's thunder.

I tried in vain one last time to get him to watch with me. "Caleb, tell me what colors you see."

"That's a green one, Daddy! And a red one!"

This lasted a minute or so before he was off tumbling down the hill again, saying, "Whoa, whoa, whoa, whoa," with each spin of his body. I started to call out to him again when Kristi leaned over to me and whispered, "Michael, just let him be a kid. There will be other years."

I was so irritated because he wouldn't sit by us and take in the fireworks. I guess I had this preconceived notion that he would sit on my lap and just squeal with delight every time one exploded. Then he would ask me if they were magic, so that his proud Daddy could stick out his chest and explain away. Luckily my understanding wife was there and was able to gently nudge me back to reality.

My expectations weren't wrong, but once again my impatience got in the way of enjoying time with my wife and sons. I should have picked up on the cues and tumbled down the hill with my boy. Fireworks have been around for hundreds of years, but my boy would be three years old for only another week.

I bet when one tumbles down the hill, lightning bugs look a lot like fireworks going off. I guess I'll have to start a new tradition on the Fourth of July. Actually, from what my three-year-old tells me, the show goes on every night!

Michael T. Powers

Over the Top

We are made to persist. That is how we find out who we are.

Tobias Wolff

My dad and I had arm wrestled for years. Sundays were typically battle days. I looked forward to testing my strength against his. When I was young and we began arm wrestling, Dad pretended to be barely able to "take me over the top." As I got older and stronger, the pretense of struggle faded, then eventually disappeared. He had to work to beat me.

The moment for the test arrived. It was halftime in the Lions game. "C'mon," he said, pointing to the floor. We found our positions on the carpet, poised to lock hands and wrists. I inhaled deeply, letting my breath out slowly. Putting on my best game face, I looked into Dad's eyes. I recognized the "Not today, kid!" stare he shot me. Even though I stood a full six inches taller than Dad, I knew his years in the paper mills had developed his muscles.

I made the first move, pulling his hand toward my straining face. The challenge was immediately met with force. My arm involuntarily drew backward, stopping just short of the floor. Aching from the awkward position of my arm, I concentrated on my right wrist. Ever so slowly, the momentum started to shift. Sweat beaded on Dad's forehead, and his face took on a deep crimson hue. The veins in his neck became pronounced. Again, I was forced back. Looking through eyes blurred by perspiration, I studied his face. This was no longer a game. Summoning every bit of remaining strength, I stopped the retreat of my arm.

We stayed locked for what seemed like hours, neither of us willing to give in. My shoulders throbbed and my back complained. My hand and wrist were numb. We had never engaged for this length of time.

Then something happened. I could almost sense the strength leaving my father; or maybe my determination multiplied my effort. I don't really know. Whatever the reason or cause, I took my dad down. Neither of us said a word. We both knew something was different now. The funny thing was that I didn't know I would feel so sad.

We never arm wrestled again.

Now as I look at my son, so young and strong in the bloom of youth, I am my dad, and I understand.

Donald Verkow

Kids and Grown-Ups:
Different as Knight and Day

You don't realize just how grown-up you really are until you have a kid.

We like to say things like "I'm a kid wrapped in an adult body" or "I feel like a kid again." But aren't we really just, *ahem*, kidding ourselves?

As much as we like to think of ourselves as kids, our bodies and our hearts are always there to remind us that we're grown-up.

I suppose I knew this all along, but the realization hit me the hardest while engaged in a little friendly jousting.

What, you don't joust? It's the hottest thing going, at least in our house.

Jousting, the competition between two knights on horseback, where one knight tries to knock the other off his mount, was a long-ago sport—about 800 years ago—equivalent to soccer in Europe or football in the United States.

Try to explain that to a toddler, though, and all you'll get is an empty stare, followed by "Come on, Daddy, joust."

So between my legs goes a makeshift horse, which is in reality a cardboard tube leftover from wrapping paper. In my right hand goes a makeshift lance, also a cardboard tube leftover from wrapping paper. I am, almost always, Bad Knight.

About thirty feet away is the condensed version of me, about three feet shorter but packing about ten times the energy. He is, almost always, Good Knight.

Our eyes meet. We raise our lances. And then in unison we call out, "Charge!"

Almost always, the battle ends with Daddy in the moat, which also happens to be the cat's water bowl. The cat is not a fan of jousting.

You do some things as a parent that when you were childless you swore you'd never do. Jousting is one such thing.

I liked thinking of myself as a kid at heart. But the lesson I've learned from jousting is that I am an adult in both body and spirit. Not only do my knees creak when I struggle to get up after being knocked down, but also I lack the heart of an honorable knight.

While I stand holding a cardboard tube between my legs, I find myself frequently turning my head, checking to see if any of the neighbors can see me through the sliding glass door.

Lately I look for excuses not to joust. "Not right now," I tell the Good Knight, "Daddy's washing dishes." Yes, I'd rather wash dishes.

The Good Knight looks down, dejected for a brief moment, but then returns his battle-worn eyes to mine with a childlike glimmer of hope and throws the dagger-like response: "After?"

Beaten once again, I sigh and surrender to his magical power over me.

After the last dish is washed, I stride to the horse stable, which is, in reality, a large wicker basket. I pull out my trusty steed and grab hold of my lance. The Good Knight beams as we square off on opposite sides of the room. Finally, we raise our makeshift lances and call out that one word the Good Knight has been waiting to hear all day: "Charge!"

Randy Richardson

The Son Also Rises

One of my friends is expecting. Technically, it's his wife who is expecting, but he is the one who is full of expectations.

You see, after two lovely girls, they are now expecting a boy. And yours truly—as the proud owner and operator of a four-year-old boy—is seen as a source of information on how having a boy in the house differs from having a girl. It's nice to be considered an expert on anything, but I'm afraid the information I have for him based on my own experience can't really be considered encouraging.

In our house, having a boy means a constant whirl of activity. I have watched in amazement when girls come to visit and they sit quietly for two hours absorbed in a coloring book. When it comes to creative projects and crafts, my son's motto is "art in thirty seconds or less." Girls rarely require you to holler about drawing on the furniture, gluing their eyelids together, or painting the dog. With girls, frequently the finished artistic product actually looks like something. My son is still in his abstract period, but unlike many modern artists, he doesn't take offense when it takes twenty guesses to figure out what he's drawn.

Parents of girls tell me their daughters have a few favorite toys that are loved and cherished and provide hours of entertainment. They even get handed down as family heirlooms. Little boys—and a lot of grown men—have attention spans that would leave room in a gnat's appointment book. My advice to the proud father-to-be is not to waste money on expensive educational toys that will be looked at once and then tossed aside with no more thought given to them than to a Libertarian candidate. When it comes to boys, the secret of toys is volume, volume, volume.

And speaking of volume, there is the noise. A house with a boy in it is a noisy house. Just eating a bowl of cereal can generate enough racket to get noise complaints from a nearby airport. I've given up trying to watch the news with the sound on. If I want to follow a TV show, I'm going to have to take up lipreading.

And no toy will ever be used in the hands of a boy for the purpose for which it was designed. Practically anything can be turned into a rocket launcher, jet fighter, or fortress, unless, of course, they already happen to be a rocket launcher, jet fighter, or fortress, in which case they will be used as something else.

Boys can be affectionate, in their own way. But be warned—boys' hugs hurt. For most little boys, unless you can hear several major bones crack, it doesn't count as a hug. Don't even get me started on good-bye kiss-related injuries.

Unlike little girls, bath time for boys holds the same excitement as a National Geographic special on predators of the Amazon. I have rarely had to let the water out of the tub when my son's bath is finished. Somehow there's never enough water left to worry about. Our bathroom floor, however, is growing moss.

Of course, "experts" will tell you that normal little boys

actually suffer from any number of behavioral issues, when what they really mean is the problem is that boys are not girls—something my friend will find out soon enough.

Stephen Lautens

Father to Son

If you think you can do a thing or think you can't do a thing, you are right.

Henry Ford

Many knots are easier to tie than the classic Double Windsor—especially for nine-year-old fingers still struggling with the intricacies of the shoelace double knot.

But when Jon got his first non-clip-on tie recently, I was determined he would learn to tie it properly. And as far as I was concerned, that meant a Double Windsor. None of this silly Half Windsor stuff for my son. No, sir. And no Four-in-Hand beginning knot, either. Walker men are Double Windsor men—or they are nothing at all.

"It's not that hard, Jon," I assured him as I quickly whipped fabric around my neck in a sequence so familiar I could do it in my sleep. "See? Around this side, back behind, then around this side, then around the front and back behind and down and through. Pull it tight—and there it is!"

I admired the perfectly straight, perfectly shaped knot with its fashionable, cute little dimple that almost seemed to smile back at me from the mirror. Then I looked at Jon's tie, hanging around his neck, over his shoulder, under his armpit, through his belt loop, and out his fly. As knots go, it was extraordinary—enough to bring tears to the eyes of the Great Houdini. But as a knot for tying a tie . . . well, it was no Double Windsor.

Jon smiled at me sheepishly. "I think I need a little help," he said.

That was like the captain of the Titanic saying he had a little ice problem. But I didn't tell Jon that. I just stepped in behind him, took the fabric of his tie into my hands, and demonstrated the knot from his perspective.

"Watch," I said. "Around this side, then back behind, then around this side . . ."

Suddenly, I was enveloped by an overwhelming feeling of déjà vu. I had experienced this simple moment of father-son sharing before—twice, in fact, once ten or twelve years ago with Jon's older brother, Joe. And once many years ago when my father stood behind me and tried to teach my clumsy hands how to tie the Double Windsor.

It wasn't pretty.

"But, Dad," I remember saying, "wouldn't it be easier to just do this?" I had tied a knot that was part Bowline, part Half-Hitch and mostly Granny.

"Well, that's a fine knot, son," Dad said as he struggled to loosen my tie from my neck, where it hung like a lopsided hangman's noose. "But . . . well, this other knot is the knot my father taught me, and I think he learned it from his father. All my brothers use it, and I've taught it to all your brothers. It's sort of the family knot—the tie that binds. So humor me, okay? Learn this knot. And then if you want to use your fancy knot instead, I'll understand."

Then Dad had stood behind me and taught me how to tie the Double Windsor—just as I was standing behind Jon and teaching him. Jon picked it up much more quickly than I had—just a few weeks later, he was tying it all by himself (I think I was asking for help until my wedding day). He may experiment with other knots through the years. I know I did (and I'm pretty sure I've seen a Half-Windsor around his big brother's neck).

But eventually I came back to the family knot, even though I'm not exactly sure why. It isn't because it's easier, because it isn't. And truth be told, it doesn't even look that much better. It's just something about that father-son thing.

The tie that binds.

Joseph Walker

The Walk of Life

Do not follow where the path may lead. Go instead where there is no path and leave a trail.

Ralph Waldo Emerson

The day is etched in my memory for so many reasons; the fact that I was actually allowed to take the day off from school stands out prominently. When my dad said that I was taking the day off, I thought something was up, something immediately was strange. He said that he had a special treat for me.

My dad has always been a hardworking man—up before the crack of dawn and home after twelve hours on the job—and he never took his vacations from the job lightly. So it was something special for Dad to call on me, the youngest of his five children, on his day off.

I will always carry with me crystalline images of shared moments between me and Dad: stopping for doughnuts after church; the first time I hit Dad's perfectly pitched fastball over the left-center field fence (after years of Dad throwing batting pratice); losing countless free-throw contests in the driveway. Even mundane things like raking leaves or going to the grocery store still hold a soft spot in my heart, but there was something different about the walks we would take that stand above all the memories.

Throughout my childhood, on every vacation the family spent at least one day hiking. Any combination of brothers and sisters would venture out into the hills of New England for a day with our dad. This was Dad's reprieve for two weeks each year, and whoever was up for the task was invited. This particular day was my day.

We didn't get a particularly early start, eating a leisurely breakfast. "We're going to go in and pick up my father. I figure we'll head out to the Quabbin and take Grandpa out to where he used to go fishing," Dad said, looking up from his newspaper. I slurped milk from my cereal bowl.

When he said we were picking up my grandfather, I suddenly realized this was indeed a special day. My grandfather had recently become ill, but this day he was well enough to get out for a walk.

We packed a bottle of water, some nuts and berries, and a first aid kit into a rucksack. When we arrived at my grandparents' house, I noticed something peculiar and pleasant in the air. *Is this what it smells like all the time I am in school?* I thought. The crisp morning was delightful. Just a few scattered puffy clouds and a gentle May breeze distinguished this day from any other warm spring morning. Worcester, Massachusetts, hadn't ever been a pleasant-smelling city, but I was doing all I could to soak in this loveliness.

My grandmother scurried about the house as best she could, fixing coffee and packing sandwiches for later in the day. I sat in a chair at the kitchen table while my grandfather collected his things. He had visibly slowed in recent months. As he sat next to me at the table, putting on his shoes, his actions were deliberate; going through the exact order of steps he had shown me when I was five and just learning to tie my own laces. Dad and I were quiet.

Once on the road, we headed our car west, traveling through tiny Massachusetts towns like Leicester, Hubbardston, and Hardwick—places that you literally had to go out of your way to pass through. I watched the road, the small-town buildings, and the trees pass by. Dad and Grandpa talked up front, quietly and only intermittently. I watched both of them, and a shiver of curiosity ran through me. It was a sensation that happened only in moments like these, when I knew something was good, when I never wanted to forget this moment—a shiver, warm and gentle, reminded me. I watched and felt the heat of the sun through the car window.

Off Route 32A, we turned onto a gravel-covered parking area, big enough for only three cars. We had not seen a car pass for the last ten minutes of the ride and no others were at this parking area, so by all indications we'd be to ourselves.

We traveled an old hardscrabble road with blades of grass growing through the cracks, past two intakes for the aqueduct system that brings water to the citizens of Boston. The sound of water rushing far below the surface was the only thing we heard other than birds and our footsteps on this day.

Grandpa told us fishing stories, and Dad talked about the eagles and pheasants he had seen the last time he'd been in the area. I stayed quiet for the most part. The history of the Quabbin Reservoir whispered to me through the woods. Four towns had been evacuated and flooded to make this water supply for the city dwellers, but something lingered in the air. It was nearly tangible. If I stayed completely still, I swear I could hear the sounds of townspeople echo off the hills.

We made the final turn and came to the water's edge. For years my grandfather had brought his boat to this launch. It wasn't without sadness that he looked at the low water and gave a slight smile. "Water's low, huh?" he asked my father. Dad nodded.

As a result of the reintroduction of bald eagles at the Quabbin Reservoir during the 1980s (eagles had been killed off in the area due to pollution and contamination of their food supply during the industrial boom earlier in the century), fishing had been reduced to all but the shoreline, and a dry winter meant the season would not open for another few weeks.

"I have a . . ." Grandpa said, reaching down, "a . . . rock, or something . . ."

Dad reached to help support him as I gave a look to Dad as if to say, "How do I help?" He told me to bend down to support Grandpa. Grandpa grabbed my shoulder and after some comedic moments of awkwardness, I helped get his shoe off and, sure enough, a pebble big enough to certainly be bothersome was in his shoe. I handed the pebble to him, and he flicked it away with some choice words. He was clearly frustrated with his inability to manage an otherwise simple task. I put his shoe back on and tied the laces, smiling while I did so, because Grandpa had helped me the same way long ago.

When I finished, and with Grandpa's shoe now comfortably in place again, Dad asked if we should head back to the car. I didn't want to head back, but I knew Grandpa was getting tired. We stood at that spot shoulder to shoulder looking over the lake and took in the view and the pleasure of being together. In the last year I had grown taller than Dad, and he stood a few inches higher than his father. We stood, three generations together in the sunlight.

Grandpa insisted we press on. We walked across the South Baffle Dam, heading west toward Mt. Zion. When we arrived at the other side, I sensed that Grandpa had come as far as he wanted to. I sensed he was very proud about his resolve to get to the edge of the woods. It was almost as if he wanted to just keep going and let nature take him back into the waiting arms of the Creator.

Dad said I could head up around the bend if I wanted. I had the awkward gait of a seventeen-year-old boy who had outgrown everyone in the family. I could easily make up the ground and Dad knew it. I seized the opportunity and ambled pensively, occasionally turning to see my heroes walking together. I stopped just after the bend and paused. Times like these call out for a prayer of thanksgiving. I said my piece and gave thanks for the blessing of my life. I looked up the trail farther, hoping to see some recognition for my prayer. Then I turned back and saw Dad and Grandpa slowly making their way back toward the car. I bounded back across the Baffle Dam.

The day at Quabbin with my father and me marked the last time my grandfather got out to his fishing spot. In real terms, it was his final walk of leisure. From that day on, everything became increasingly difficult. Old age crept in rather quickly and a stroke took its toll. Grandpa passed away within the year.

I learned more that day about myself and about the world around me than I did in all my years of schooling. Life wasn't about facts, it wasn't about dates, and it certainly wasn't about Advanced Algebra. I learned that day about the way life is on the good days—the texture and essence of the best life has to offer. I glimpsed myself on that day. I saw myself in Dad. I saw Dad in Grandpa, and I saw Grandpa in both Dad and me. Imprints, gifts from the generations that preceded me, reside deep within my person. I understood these subtleties on that day, more so than any other day before or since.

As I now stand at the precipice of parenthood myself, I live each day with this memory emblazoned in my soul, and I know I will share a special day with my children, just as my dad shared one with me.

Matthew Favreault

Pinewood Derby

The Pinewood Derby race fast approached in my son's Cub Scout den, so you know what that meant for a handy guy like me: updating the homeowners insurance.

I had all of the neat power tools a dad would need to make a classic Pinewood Derby car. And I knew how to plug every one of them into the socket.

It got tricky after that.

So, needless to say, when my son received his rectangular block of solid wood, four wheels, and four nails to hold the wheels in place, he stared up at me with those hero-worshipping eyes that said, "What masterpiece are we going to build, Dad?" I went right for the rules.

"What are you looking for?" my wife asked. "The rules on how much a dad can do to help build the car?"

"No," I answered, "the rules on how much a dad can pay to purchase one on eBay."

"Oh, won't that be lovely," she said. "I can hear it now. On race night, when the Cubmaster goes around the room asking the boys what part they played in the design and build of their Pinewood Derby cars, our son can say that he typed in your credit card number. Maybe there's a patch for that?"

I got the point. I also explained I was inept with tools.

But she reminded me that our son had his hopes pinned on making a car, and as his father, it was my responsibility to help him realize that dream.

So first, I tried the easy approach.

"What are we going to make, Dad?" my son asked as we walked ceremoniously into the garage.

A wide, dramatic smile spread across my face (the same I used when telling him the doctor's shot wouldn't hurt). "This," I said as I pulled the uncut block of wood from the original box and held it above my head.

My son's face sank. "A block of wood?"

"Yep," I said excitedly.

"We aren't going to cut it and sand it and put in a steering wheel?"

"We don't need to," I explained. "Now, don't scream for joy too loud and frighten the neighbors, but this block of wood is really . . . now brace yourself . . . a *runaway train.*"

His face brightened. "Cool! You mean a steam engine with cowcatcher and smokestack?"

"No, silly," I said, maintaining my enthusiasm. "I mean a boxcar with Southern and Pacific."

After my son stopped crying, I switched to Plan B: making a sports car. Several hours later, my wife walked into the garage.

"You've been working on that car all of this time?" she asked, looking at her watch.

I nodded. "All except the two times I drove to the Boy Scout store to purchase more Pinewood Derby kits."

She studied my efforts. "What are you making?"

"Guess," I said, holding up the near-finished car.

"It looks like driftwood."

"Because it's smooth and sleek?"

"No, because it's bent."

Plan C called for sending my son to his grandpa's house with a new Pinewood Derby kit. They made a beautiful car.

Later, my wife told me it was okay that I'm not handy—
she said I did plenty of good things with our son. She also
said to look on the bright side.

"Which was?" I asked.

"We now have kindling for the fireplace."

I wonder if power tools burn, too?

Ken Swarner

The Giants

It's not whether you get knocked down, it's whether you get up.

Vince Lombardi

My stepson was in his first year of T-ball. All the teams were named after professional teams. We lived in the San Diego area and our team was the Padres, so all the boys recognized the name. And by and large all their fathers, stepfathers, older brothers, and grandpas knew the Padres, as well as every other team in the majors.

The last practice before the first game was just coming to a close. The coach called the boys in to sit against the backstop. He handed out uniforms and gave the team last-minute instructions. He told them to wear their new uniforms and that they were playing the Giants in an 8:00 AM game. He told them to get there a half hour early to warm up, and he estimated how long the game would take. As he finished his instructions, the boys became uncharacteristically quiet. Dads on the scene wondered at this sudden stillness. The boys had always been so enthusiastic about every game.

Eventually, the coach noticed the subdued mood of the team, so he asked if they had any questions. The boys looked at one another as if to say, "*You* ask him." The coach and dads looked at the boys as if to say, "What the heck's going on here?"

Finally, one little boy, tears filling his eyes, asked, "How can we play giants? We're just little kids!"

I'm sure more than one little boy stayed in the car the next morning until he saw at least one (pint-size) player from the "Giants." And plenty of dads, those who hadn't already heard, wondered what the heck was up with their sons.

Michael Fulton

8

THE WISDOM OF ALL AGES

An old Cherokee was teaching his grandson about life. "A fight is going on inside me," he said to the boy. "It is a terrible fight and it is between two wolves. One is evil—he is anger, envy, sorrow, regret, greed, arrogance, self-pity, guilt, resentment, inferiority, lies, false pride, superiority, and ego. The other is good— he is joy, peace, love, hope, serenity, humility, kindness, benevolence, empathy, generosity, truth, compassion, and faith. This same fight is going on inside you—and inside every other person, too."

The grandson thought about it for a minute and then asked his grandfather, "Which wolf will win?"

The old Cherokee simply replied, "The one you feed."

Indian Fable

"I know the difference between right and
wrong—it's the similarities that mix me up."

Hands of Time

And in the end, it's not the years in your life that count. It's the life in your years.

Abraham Lincoln

I looked at the hand resting on the table; it looked familiar. Slightly pale, lacking the heavy tan of earlier years and earlier seasons, and now a few brown spots seemed to make their presence known. I stared at it for a minute as I answered my cell phone, surely not a polite thing to do, to talk on the phone at the dinner table.

No one seemed to notice, though, as I quietly chatted my way through dinner. I looked at the fingers, slightly crooked, seeming more crooked than I had remembered, and the nails, perfectly cleaned and trimmed. They'd always been that way, I surmised, the impeccable habit of a man who washes his hands a hundred times a day. But the age spots bothered me. When had those hands reached that milestone, that acknowledgement of decades of service?

Still, they were good-looking hands, I thought, ivory skin against the crisp white dress shirt, a gold watchband slightly visible beneath the starched cuff.

Grasping the water glass with a firm, steady grip, it was a hand that looked as if it could tell many a tale. The thumbnail was not quite perfect, showing signs of having been smashed one too many times when younger, perhaps with a hammer as he missed the other nail, the nail he was trying to pound into a piece of wood. The skin on the thumb was rough-looking as well, the result of a new piece of glass that didn't cut exactly the way it was supposed to many years ago, and a piece of thumb lost in the process.

No ring on the fingers of the right hand, but I glanced at the left one holding a fork. On that one the soft shine of a well-worn gold wedding band filled a groove on the third finger, a groove so deep it looked as though it had been there from birth. And an age spot or two on that hand as well, I noticed.

I thought of those hands as I talked, and continued to study them. Hands tell us so much about a person's life. I pictured these hands on a younger man, whose hands carried a baseball or a football, or packed snow into a tight ball before winging it wildly, that also grasped a shovel or a rake and pushed a lawnmower around the backyard. In my mind I saw two hands clasped together tightly, as young lovers do when they walk, the rough one holding a smaller, softer one. I pictured the hands of a young father picking up his newborn son, gently fastening the snaps on a toddler's overalls, or teaching a youngster to tie his shoes.

I thought of the work those hands had done: bagging groceries, pumping gas, working on machinery large and small. Countless hours and miles spent grasping a steering wheel, and in later years, the incessant pecking at a computer keyboard.

I wondered, did he ever think that these hands would get this old, that his fingers would ache from the stiffness in the almost worn-out joints, and that without gloves he would not be able stand even the mildest of winter's days?

I doubted it, for seldom does anyone think he will get old until his body starts to slow, and perhaps also his mind, until he lacks the acuity, both mentally and physically, that gave him the edge he used to have.

I thought of my father and his hands, and remembered his smooth gold ring, worn soft from years of exposure to the work he had done. My father's hands lifted me when I was young. One of my fondest memories is of Dad picking me up and putting me on his shoulders as he stood chest deep in the cool water of Cayuga Lake, and then letting me dive forward over his head. I would beg him to do it over and over, part of our summertime Sunday afternoons.

And I thought of Dad's hands in his later years, watching him absently massage his fingers as he talked, the fingers that ached often and were always cold. He would sit in his chair in the late evenings, tired from a full day of work, his hands covered with a little blanket, trying in vain to keep them warm.

I looked at the hands on the table once more. My father's hands, for sure, just the way I remember them, only they are attached to my arms now. I finished the phone conversation with my son, a conversation spanning nearly thirty years and 2,000 miles, and while wondering where time had gone, thanked him for sharing my solitary evening meal.

Gary B. Xavier

The Invitation

Three things in human life are important. The first is to be kind. The second is to be kind. And the third is to be kind.

Henry James

We sit close together, bouncing along in the tow truck. Our eyes absorb dashboard knobs, dials, and levers. The CB radio noises amuse us. We laugh at the cars below us in freeway traffic. We enjoy riding high.

"This is neat, Dad!" My son's voice radiates joy. And I hug him. How often does a father enjoy a ride in the vehicle of his son's dreams? Often enough? Never mind that my car has broken down.

At age nine, impatient for school to end and summer vacation to begin, he says, "Dad, can we go camping soon?"

We pitch our tent on a bluff overlooking a little lake in a beautiful valley. During the day, we fish for largemouth bass, which we would catch and release if we were to catch some. At night, we keep the tent flap open and look at the sky.

"Oh, neat!" my son exclaims with each shooting star. We make our private wishes.

The night sky entertains him until he falls asleep, secure in his sleeping bag beside mine. Our good time together under the stars goes all too quickly.

"I didn't ask to live here," he reminds me.

"You keep that attitude and you won't be," I inform him.

Who is this child who has come to live with me at age sixteen? Why are we adversaries? Does the divorce still trouble him? Is someone at school picking on him? He doesn't say.

Regardless, he's mine and he's precious to me, but he does make me wonder how someone who was once so close can now be so emotionally distant.

The prodigal son stage lasts only a year.

It seems like forever.

Now years older, I get a call. "Dad, you always say we should be careful what we ask for, because we may get it." My son is sitting on the couch with his girlfriend. He has my attention. He has trained me to be patient with him and to keep my heart and mind open.

"You've been asking for a grandchild," he says. "I am here to tell you that we are going to make you a grandpa. What do you think of that?"

My heart goes *ka-thump*.

Stunned, ecstatic, surprised, *very* surprised, fighting back tears and trying to keep from dancing a jig, I stay calm and hand out congratulations.

"I proposed and she accepted!" He nearly shouts into the telephone. "Dad, I want you to be the first one to know that when we get back to California, we will be getting married!"

He is calling late at night from Ohio. I had complained that I was always the last one to know what was going on in my son's life. He took that to heart. Now he is sharing his major moment with me first. He still has no idea how precious he is to me.

Fatherhood begins for my son with cutting the cord in the delivery room. He immediately bonds with his daughter. A gentleness and deep compassion surround him in his fatherly duties. Using a voice more mellow than any he ever heard from me, he cleans, feeds, and nurtures his daughter. I marvel at my son's parenting skills and hold him in awe.

He balances family life with his college work and first earns a bachelor degree and a year later a master of science degree. Such achievements are unheard of in our family tree.

Despite his full schedule and long hours, he takes time to send a letter home that ends with, "I hope to fish for largemouth bass with you soon. Maybe we'll catch one this time."

I like my son.

"And I won't see you for three years. Right?"

"Not unless you come to Germany," my son says.

"Your wife is four months' pregnant," I remind him.

"Dad," he says, as if he's the adult, "babies are born in Germany all the time."

I make one last try. "Well, are you coming back to California?"

He takes a deep breath, and then he says in the mellow voice he uses on his daughter, "We haven't planned that far ahead."

Long pause.

When he was a little boy, we would hold hands when we walked together. Back then, I could also pick him up and hug him. By the end of grade school, however, he had stopped hand-holding with me, but a hug had become traditional.

I reach up and hug him. "I love you, son." He hugs me back.

"I love you, Dad."

"I'll miss you, son."

"I'll miss you, Dad."

He drives off and leaves me with my thoughts: *Why*

didn't I tell him he had turned out all right and that I am proud of him? With a few more words he would have known I loved who he is as a person, not what he does, like his volunteer work in kindergarten class. Just him. Unconditionally. I didn't say that because all I could think of was that he had been home a year and not once did we fish for a largemouth bass.

His postcard arrives and I sit on the porch with it a long time and look with my eyes and my mind at my son's adventurous life. He's rock climbing, the card says, visiting towns whose names I can't pronounce, and learning a different language. Whoever he is now, he's doing a good job of living his life.

In my son's house, he is thought of as a husband and father, and soon another little person will arrive and call him "Daddy." He's a package deal, now. He belongs to all of us, technically, but more so to the family he created. The distance between father and son is increasing, naturally and respectfully.

We'll get close to each other again, but we'll never really close the entire distance between us. He's over there in his world, a place I've never been. Future times together will be visits by invitation. We won't live together under the same roof anymore, maybe not even in the same town or state. And that's okay. We've ridden the tow truck together, made our wishes on shooting stars, and we've fished together. Catch and release is our style.

Gibran once said of children: *Their souls dwell in the house of tomorrow, which you cannot visit, not even in your dreams.*

The philosopher is right about the house of tomorrow business, but with a passport I'll visit my son's house in Germany in June.

I have an invitation.

John J. Lesjack

Just a Little Bit Longer

His thick wavy hair was as white as freshly fallen snow; he more than once won the "Mr. Snowflake" title at the Senior Citizens Club. With a smile as childlike as a cherub's, he possessed the wisdom of a modern-day Socrates. Unknown beyond his own community, the obscure humanitarian touched the lives of those close to him, warmly, like the wings of an angel.

This man could be someone familiar to you. Perhaps that cheerful neighbor who greets you with a friendly wave each time you cross paths. Or that amicable fellow who waits each morning, like clockwork, for no one in particular as he sits on a park bench. Maybe he is a member of your religious congregation, the gentleman who sits in the third pew each Sunday, greeting all with a warm "Good morning." However you know him, he is a gentle presence, a comforting sense of kindred humanity.

Perhaps the attributes of this gentleman personify your significant childhood role model. In my case, I am blessed to refer to the soft-spoken man who held a unique and cherished spot in my heart—an altruistic and reassuring man who became the definition of what a man should aspire to be. I called him Father.

My father expressed patience and genuine regard for his fellow man through simple words and quiet actions. He was not loquacious; rather, he would sit quietly and listen attentively to friends, neighbors, and even strangers. Rarely offering platitudes or advice, he most often extended a simple but heartfelt "What can I do to help?" His sincere desire to lighten one's burden and share another's cross epitomized his genuine nature. It was his way of life.

As a young man, my father worked on the docks in the Brooklyn Navy Yard. His words "Just a little bit longer" encouraged his colleagues through yet another grueling day of labor. And when in a catastrophic accident a heavy load fell from a forklift and crushed the legs of his coworker, it was my father who knelt by his side while waiting for medical help, urging "Just a little bit longer, Tony."

When as a child I suffered from pneumonia and a high fever that lasted for days, he gently whispered the soothing words, "Just a little bit longer, Freddie."

Years later when my mother lay dying of cancer in the hospital, her breathing labored, he held her hand as the end approached and selflessly comforted, "Just a little bit longer, Stephie."

When my father spoke the words "Just a little bit longer," they took on a virtuous significance. They were not a hollow response a parent might use to appease an impatient child who eagerly awaits arrival at an amusement park. His words carried an unmistakable message of compassion and a willingness to lend his strength, come what may. My father's legacy is clear: Share a cross and ease a burden whenever possible. Be willing to forge lasting bonds. Cherish relationships with others in this uncertain world. In so doing, you may envision the colors in the rainbow borne from compassion.

Several years ago, I made my last trip to visit my father. At eighty-three his health was failing. One evening as the hour grew late, he said he wanted to stay up "just a little bit longer." We reminisced about my brothers' and my childhood antics. He shared stories about his own mischievous youth as well as fond memories of my mother. He clearly recounted moments of triumph and strife in his life. Then he imparted his greatest piece of wisdom: "Through it all, Freddie, the only thing that matters in life is to do all the good you can, for all the people you can, as long as you ever can."

As another Father's Day approaches, I am thankful I had the time to know my father "just a little bit longer."

Frederick Bakowski

"I know one shoulder is lower than the other. It's because my father's guiding hand is on that shoulder."

Rediscovered Hero

I don't look a thing like my father.

In his prime he had a full head of gloriously red hair; mine is sort of a mousey, dishwater blond-brown-blah. He has bright, penetrating blue eyes; mine are a nondescript hazel (no matter how big your box of crayons is, you won't find a crayon called "hazel"—I promise). He has a proud, prominent, almost Romanesque nose; mine is a squishy little blob in the middle of my face. And even at ninety-three, he has broad shoulders, strong arms, and large, powerful hands; my shoulders are narrow, my arms are reedlike, and my hands are soft, almost feminine.

Not that there is anything wrong with feminine hands. They look great on women. But they don't look virile. Like my dad's.

That is why I was startled when an older gentleman stopped me in the mall the other day.

"Aren't you Bud Walker's son?" he asked.

"Yes, I am," I said. "I'm his youngest son, Joe."

"I thought so," the gentleman said. "He used to speak of you often."

Now, you need to know that it has been years since Dad has spoken to anyone about anything. Time and disability have robbed him of one of his greatest natural abilities: communication. Dad had a way with words and a way with people that I always admired and wanted to emulate. These days Dad is in a care center, where his warm smile and pleasant disposition endear him to all he meets.

But he isn't talking—about me or anything else.

So after bringing the gentleman in the mall up-to-date with my father's condition, I had to ask him how he could, after so many years, remember Dad—not to mention Dad's youngest son.

The man paused, then said simply, "Your father is one of my heroes."

I could understand that. Dad was my hero, too. But somehow in caring for him through his current difficulties I had forgotten the bright, vibrant, charismatic man he once was.

Until a stranger reminded me.

"Years ago when I was starting out in the life insurance business, your father took me under his wing," he explained. "He taught me how to sell, but more important, he taught me how to serve my clients and develop relationships of trust and understanding with them. I've tried to run my business that way ever since. I couldn't have done it any other way.

"But that isn't the real reason your dad is my hero," the man continued. "One time a group of us from the main office went to a convention in Las Vegas. I had never been on one of these trips, but I had heard stories, you know? And sure enough, that first night a group of the guys were making plans to go places and do things that . . . well, married men shouldn't do.

"I wanted to be one of the guys, but I didn't want to do this. So I asked, 'Is Bud going?' The other guys kind of looked at one another and laughed. One of them said, 'Bud's a great guy and everything, but he doesn't know how to relax and have a good time.'

"That's all I needed to hear. I just smiled at the guy and said, 'You know what? Neither do I.' I figured if your dad could have a career without compromising his values, so could I.

"I've had a good career," the man concluded, "and in two months my wife and I are going to celebrate our fiftieth wedding anniversary. Following your Dad's example has been part of both."

I didn't find what I was looking for at the mall that day. But I found something even better: a rediscovered hero.

Even if I don't look a thing like him.

Joseph Walker

The Grandpa Who Became a Daddy

The important thing is this: To be able at any moment to sacrifice what we are for what we could become.

Charles Dubois

One thing's for sure: when you marry a man seventeen years older than you, a man who's about an inch away from his fiftieth birthday, the subject of *more* children doesn't crop up in normal conversation. His six children and my three from our previous marriages were quite enough, thank you. But surprise, surprise, a year later, our birth control bit the dust and the rabbit died with a silly grin on its face.

When the pregnancy test came back positive, I was a little hesitant to tell Harold. Hesitant? I was terrified. How do you tell a man who's dreaming of early retirement that he's about to bring into the world a member of the college graduating class of the year 2002—and the 1980s haven't even started yet?

Almost apologetically I broke the news. The way Harold responded, you'd have thought he was a thirty-year-old who'd been trying to father his first child for years. That very afternoon he rushed out to buy cigars and started handing them out to his friends.

Perhaps he thought about how babies bring a feeling of perpetual youth. Or maybe he thought that having one of our own would really solidify our marriage. He'd probably seen that old Lucille Ball movie *Yours, Mine and Ours.* Perhaps he was just glad he still had what it takes to become a father. Whatever it was, dear Harold stomped through the tulips with glee when I told him the news.

For the first two and a half years after we were married, Harold's job kept him in Wisconsin during the week, while my three children and I continued to live in northern Illinois. Of course we were together every weekend, but when I became pregnant, my heart broke when I learned the childbirth classes at our local hospital were only on Tuesday nights. Harold had not been present during the birth of his other six children, and I wanted him to experience the incredible joy and miracle of childbirth. But unless he took childbirth classes, the hospital staff wouldn't consider him fit for delivery room duty.

Undaunted by the miles and the three-hour drive between us, Harold signed up to take childbirth classes by himself at a large hospital in Milwaukee. There he was, fifty-one years old, grandfather to six, graying around the temples, sitting alone on the floor week after week, learning how to pant and blow, pant and blow. He had to do some pretty fast talking to convince his classmates he even *had* a pregnant wife.

When Andrew was born, Harold was a trouper. He coached and encouraged me through labor. In the delivery room he all but delivered the baby himself . . . even talked the doctor into letting him cut the umbilical cord.

For a man who had paced the hospital halls during the birth of his other children, I was extremely proud of his delivery-room technique. He held our son, posed for pictures, and developed a bond with Andrew within minutes of his birth.

As Andrew grew I noticed that although Harold did not get down on the floor and roughhouse with his son as much as a younger man might, he and Andrew maintained that closeness initiated at birth.

Harold survived the terrible twos and the temper-tantrum threes better than I did. Perhaps it was innate grandfatherly wisdom learned from watching his half-dozen grandkids that reminded him that all stages, no matter how exasperating, eventually pass.

Harold also remembered what it was like when his first brood was at home. Trying to support six children under eleven years of age on a 1950's teaching salary of about $5000 a year gave him ulcers. But as a newly promoted high school principal, he didn't have to worry whether or not his paycheck would cover the grocery bills.

When Andrew started school, his dad entered a new phase of life: senior citizen discounts. But in spite of his advancing years, Harold had no trouble keeping up with the younger generation. In the summer he and Andrew visited the zoo, took walks along the lake, and played catch. In the winter Harold instructed Andrew on the fine points of giving Dad good back and foot rubs in front of the TV. Andrew's reward was usually a big bowl of popcorn and then a piggyback ride to bed.

Naturally, some days Andrew put a viselike strain on Harold's good nature, such as when Andrew hauled out his toy guitar and drums and made like Buddy Holly during the ball game on TV or during one of Harold's favorite old-time movies. Or when Andrew's unbridled energy and unreserved playtime sound effects broke the sound barrier. But then those were the times Andrew drove me up a skinny-limbed tree, too . . . so Harold's age was not a factor.

Sometimes, though, Harold thought wistfully about retirement. Many of his contemporaries were planning to retire in four or five years. They talked about traveling and taking life easy. The words *condominium, Sun City,* and *motor home* punctuated their conversations. But not Harold. As he approached sixty, he was still traveling to Little League games, music lessons, parent-teacher meetings, and the orthodontist.

Often when Harold ran into an old friend, the conversation usually went something like this:

"This little guy your grandson, Harry?"

"No, this is Andrew, my son."

"Oh, ya? Heh, heh, heh."

Harold just laughed it off. Sometimes he laughed so hard he cried. Sometimes he just said, "Why me, Lord?"

All things considered, I have to say that a man in his fifties who is already a father and stepfather can definitely father a child with little worry about whether or not he can handle it. Harold always remembered the old saying about "Age is simply a matter of mind. If you don't mind, it doesn't matter."

When Andrew was nine years old, his sixty-one-year-old dad died of leukemia, a disease that can strike at any age. But in spite of losing his father at a young age, Andrew has good memories of his older dad . . . the Grandpa who became a Daddy . . . and loved every minute of it.

Patricia Lorenz

Morning Peace

It's never too late to be what we might have been.

George Eliot

As I sit here watching my two little boys sleep, tears well up in my eyes: tears of joy, pain, pride, hardship, and sacrifice. I am reminded of the obstacles I had to overcome. Most of my youthful goals were preoccupied with making money, and with creating an image of who I wanted others to see. That all changed a year ago when I quit my job and took an easier, lesser-paying, lower-status, more-time-at-home job.

I was becoming everything I had wanted to be, and yet deep down I knew if I continued on that road I would end up being nothing to my wife or children. In my profession I saw a lot of single mothers rearing children without fathers. Sometimes I'm embarrassed for my sex—men who have abandoned their children and the women who love and need them.

But I was heading down this same path, thinking that by working more, I would be providing better for my family. I was unconsciously leaving them behind. Then one day we were all in our car on a mountainous, curvy road when an oncoming, out-of-control, fully loaded fuel truck came over the ridge and crossed uncontrolled into our lane. A pullout just happened to be at the very spot we were. Along most of that road was either a cliff or a mountainside, but here was this pullout I could steer into, allowing the semi to roll past us in our lane. For some reason, we were spared that day.

Sometime during that week I realized that I had spent too many years searching for the wrong things. I had everything I ever needed right here: an incredible wife who loved me and two children who thought I was Superman.

Sitting here, watching them sleep, I realize I have made peace with my ambitions. I no longer yearn for a fast motorcycle, an exciting, dangerous career, an image of wealth and accomplishment based on material goods. No, I'm quite happy being *Dad*.

I left that fast-paced career and went back to my old, safe, monotonous job. I have a lot more time with my wife and kids now, and I still struggle to get along sometimes, to communicate instead of yell, to talk instead of accuse. But I've finally made peace with it all, and it feels so good to sit here and finally be able to cry, because I know now that I have the greatest responsibility a man can ever have. I have the responsibility of being a husband and a father, and I love that.

Andy Radujko

The Winner

Not everything that can be counted counts, and not everything that counts can be counted.

Albert Einstein

When my oldest son was twelve, he expressed a great interest in the local bike races, which ran every Sunday during the summer. On Sunday afternoons we attended the races, and after watching for a period of time, he decided to get into the action. Each new participant was allowed one day of racing before being required to become a member. So I signed him up, pinned on his number, and with a borrowed helmet he was off and racing.

As the early heats ran, I could proudly see that he was one of the top three racers in each heat. This meant if all went well, he would be in the finals, and with some good effort could very well take home the winning trophy.

During the races he had made friends with another racer, and between heats they could be found talking and pointing at sprockets and various bike parts like a pair of seasoned racers. I kept my distance since this was his day, and I only lent a hand when necessary. I bought both boys lunch, and we got ready for the afternoon races. My son and his newfound friend were in the top two positions all afternoon, with each of them winning their heats with reasonable ease.

Then it was time for the final race of the day to determine the overall winner. I beamed with pride as his name was announced on the loudspeaker and he took his place with the top eight racers of the day.

When the gate dropped, the eight boys launched themselves down the ramp and into the first turn, legs pumping furiously and looks of determination barely visible behind full helmets, oblivious to the cloud of dust and the roar from the bleachers.

Around the second turn and over the bumps the bikes bounded into the air as though they were spring loaded, over the table top, through more turns and bumps, and down the home stretch. My son's friend crossed the finish line in the lead with my son not half a bike length behind.

When the dust had settled and the trophies awarded, we loaded up his bike, and with his second-place trophy clutched proudly in his hand, we headed home. After much praise and discussion and a stop at the local ice cream shop, we finally turned into our driveway and stopped. I said, "I thought you rode well all day; however, I couldn't help but notice you seemed a little off during the last race. I thought you could have won and had the big trophy."

"Dad, that boy doesn't have any parents," was his only reply.

I could not have been prouder.

Calvin Riendeau

Going Fishing with Grandpa

"And who is this a picture of?" asked the teacher, Miss James, as she studied the first-grade student's response to her question: "Who is the most important person in the world?"

"My grandpa," the six-year-old boy replied matter-of-factly, as though it were so obvious no answer should have been required.

"Your grandpa?" said Miss James in wonderment. "All of your classmates drew portraits of the president of the United States. Your grandpa must be very special."

"Yeah, he's pretty neat."

To be honest, the thought of drawing a portrait of the president of the United States had never crossed the small boy's mind. In fact, he wondered why his friends had not drawn pictures of their grandpas. Didn't they know that recess, fishing, and grandpas were three of the greatest inventions of all time? After all, where was the president of the United States when the small boy hooked his first bluegill? His first largemouth bass? It wasn't the president who had patiently shown the boy how to bait a fishhook and tie a leader. Or how to gently release a fish back into the water. Certainly the president had never stopped what he was doing to calmly help the boy untangle a web of line in a backlash spinning reel. It wasn't the president who had taught the boy other important things he needs to know—important things like how to skip flat stones across the water, how to whistle, how to play Crazy Eights and checkers, and how to hammer nails without bending them. The president never gave the boy a hand-crafted wooden toolbox for his fifth birthday or made him a "ginchy" fiberglass fly rod of his very own or even taught him funny old-fashioned words like "ginchy," which means "cool." To be sure, the president definitely wasn't ginchy like the small boy's grandpa. The president also didn't tell stories about what the small boy's dad was like when he was a boy. Stories that always made the grandson laugh—imagine his dad once being "a little squirt," too! No, the small boy could not fancy spending an entire summer afternoon under "the great, big hydrogen bomb in the sky"—that's what his grandpa called the sun—standing side by side with the president of the United States, patiently waiting for a fish to make a red-and-white bobber dance wildly. Nor could he imagine watching the president tie delicate fishing flies for hours on end in a basement fantasyland of tools and thingamabobs and endless jars filled with fishhooks, feathers and fur, and other various fly-tying doodads.

"Hey, Grandpa, how come you don't just use worms like I do?" the boy once asked while "helping" his grandpa tie a fly.

"Oh, it takes a mighty skillful fisherman like yourself to catch a fish with a worm," came the answer. "That's why you always catch all those big fish while I catch the little ones. I'd better stick to using flies if I want to have a chance to keep up with you."

"Okay, Grandpa. But if you change your mind, I'll share my worms with you."

The president probably didn't even know how to tie a nymph fly or skewer a worm onto a hook so it wouldn't fall off as soon as it hit the water. Maybe the president didn't even like to fish—now there was a thought!

But the little boy did and so did his grandpa. They also liked to watch Westerns and Marx Brothers movies and baseball games. Yes, they were a perfect pair, these two.

"Which way is the wind blowing?" the little boy would impatiently ask about every two minutes during the perfect pair's hike to a farmer's pond or a lily pad–surfaced lake. Before answering, the grandpa would stop and moisten his finger in his mouth, then extend the wet index high in the air, all the while the grandson mimicking him. Upon seeing which side of his finger-turned-weather-vane dried first, the grandpa would smile and respond, "I do believe it's blowing from the west."

Always, the wind blew from the west. Always, this excited the fisherboy who would then recite by heart a poem his grandpa had taught him:

> When the wind is from the north,
> The wise fisherman does not go forth.
> When the wind is from the south,
> It blows the hook into the fish's mouth.
> When the wind is from the east,
> 'Tis not fit for man nor beast.
> But when the wind is from the west,
> The fishing is the very best.

The fisherboy is now a fisherman who misses "the most important person in the world," who passed away many years ago. In his honor he likes to grab his grandpa's old favorite red felt ginchy fishing hat to keep the great, big hydrogen bomb in the sky from burning his scalp and goes fishing. Usually he takes along his own fisherboy-son, and sometimes his fisherman-father. Oh, yes. The fisherboy-turned-man always takes along his grandpa's old creel, too—in case the wind is blowing from the west.

Woody Woodburn

I'll Tell Him Tomorrow

When my boy was a baby, as small as can be,
I'd hold him so tightly, quite certain he'd see,
How happy I was having him as my son,
Sure that watching him grow would be lots of fun.

I'll tell him tomorrow, I'd say in my mind,
"This blue bundle of joy is really a find.
I'll tell him I love him," when he'll understand,
When he's a bit older, we'll talk man to man.

Although only three, he valiantly tried,
To hold back the tears, when his grandmother died.
He stayed by her side, right up to the end,
Kissing and hugging her, hoping she'd mend.

I'll tell him tomorrow, I'd say in my brain,
"That compassion is something that can not be feigned.
I'll tell him I love him," when he'll understand,
When he's a bit older, we'll talk man to man.

In a blink of an eye, he was leaving for school,
Though just kindergarten, I wept like a fool.

He shared and helped others, and his teacher would
    praise
Just how special he was, in so many ways . . .

I'll tell him tomorrow, I'd say in my mind,
"I'm proud he's so patient, so friendly and kind.
"I'll tell him I love him," when he'll understand,
When he's a bit older, we'll talk man to man.

A new baby was born, a pretty, sweet girl,
And I knew from that moment that she'd be his pearl.
He'd protect her from harm, and not let her down,
He'd play with her endlessly, with nary a frown.

I'll tell him tomorrow, I'd think in my head,
"He thinks not of himself, but of his sister instead.
I'll tell him I love him," when he'll understand,
When he's a bit older, we'll talk man to man.

As he played different sports, like baseball for one,
He'd win some and lose some, but always had fun.
It was real hard to tell if he won or he lost;
He never cried or complained—no equipment was
    tossed.

I'll tell him tomorrow, I'd say very softly,
"That he's a good sport," a trait I hold lofty.
"I'll tell him I love him," when he'll understand,
When he's a bit older, we'll talk man to man.

He's tall, almost twelve, and it's hard to remember,
The small baby boy, born after September.
His compassion is boundless, he has a good heart.
His kind acts add up, too many to chart.

I'll tell him tomorrow, I said, not aloud,
"How the way that's he's grown has made me quite
   proud.
I'll be glad I'm his father, until the end of my days."
I'll tell him I love him in so many ways.

Then I turned on the news, and saw a man in great pain,
He was driving his car, in the strong, pouring rain.
He had lost all control and ran into a tree.
His son had rode with him and was killed instantly.

Had that father told his son that he loved him a lot?
Or had he thought, "There's no worry. Time is one thing
   I've got."
I thought of my son, and the things I should say.
I decided right then, "I'll tell him today."

                                        Lanny Zechar

It's Good to Be Here

*Be kind, for everyone you meet is fighting a
hard battle.*

Plato

A gentle autumn breeze ruffled my father's white wispy
hair. The rugged mountains behind him, resplendent in
their fall colors, framed his face in vivid reds, golds, and
yellows. He squinted his one good eye against the bright
midday sunshine.

And he smiled.

I'd like to be able to tell you what he was smiling about.
It could have been the fresh air, or the sunshine, or the fact
that tapioca pudding was waiting for him back inside the
care center. It could have been any one of those things, or
all of them, or none of them. I'll never know. Alzheimer's
doesn't allow for a lot of explanation.

So we sat there, Dad in his wheelchair and I on a park
bench, holding hands and looking out over a pleasant,
peaceful October morning. I asked him how he was feeling, and he said, "Fine." I asked if the people at the care
center were taking good care of him, and he said, "Yes." I

told him about the birth of my second granddaughter, and how we are anxiously awaiting the arrival of another grandchild in March.

And he smiled.

At last I stood to begin the walk back to the care center. As I stooped to release the brakes on Dad's wheelchair, he reached up with a shaky hand and touched my cheek. I looked into his eyes. They were focused. Concentrated. He struggled to speak.

"It's . . . it's . . . good . . ."

I wasn't sure whether to wait and let him finish or to try to help him. During the past year or two, his ability to communicate has diminished significantly. I can't remember the last time I heard him utter a coherent sentence of more than a word or two. And yet, he seemed to be working so hard to say something. I had to help.

"What's good, Dad? The weather? The park? The care center? What's good?"

He seemed to gather himself for one last push.

"Here," he said. "To . . . be . . . here."

His struggle ended. His message was out there. But what was it?

"It's good to be here?" I asked. "Is that what you're trying to say? It's good to be here?"

And he smiled.

I took his frail hands in mine and kissed him on the forehead.

"Yes, it is, Dad," I said, tears surging to my eyes. "It's good to be here."

I considered his message as we strolled back to the care center. If any man has a right to complain about his current lot in life, it is my father. He had led a good and honorable life filled with love, service, and sacrifice. To be suffering the indignities of this disease at a time when he should be savoring the fruits of his labors seems patently unfair. And yet, in that one moment of clarity and comprehension, his one thought is that—despite everything—"It's good to be here."

I've thought about that in relation to my own life lately, and I've decided that Dad, as usual, is right. Despite the struggles, fears, and challenges that daily surround us, it's good to be here. It's good to be alive. It's good to experience all that life offers—the good things and the bad, the triumphs and the tragedies, the joys and the vicissitudes. It's good to be here even when it's bad to be here, because that's when we learn and grow the most.

I tried to explain all of that to Dad the next time I saw him.

And he smiled.

Joseph Walker

More Chicken Soup?

Many of the stories and poems you have read in this book were submitted by readers like you who had read earlier Chicken Soup for the Soul books. We publish many Chicken Soup for the Soul books every year. We invite you to contribute a story to one of these future volumes.

Stories may be up to twelve hundred words and must uplift or inspire. You may submit an original piece, something you have read, or your favorite quotation on your refrigerator door.

To obtain a copy of our submission guidelines and a listing of upcoming Chicken Soup books, please write, fax, or check our website.

Please send your submissions to:

Chicken Soup for the Soul
Website: www.chickensoup.com
P.O. Box 30880
Santa Barbara, CA 93130
Fax: 805-563-2945

We will be sure that both you and the author are credited for your submission.

For information about speaking engagements, other books, audiotapes, workshops, and training programs, please contact any of our authors directly.

Supporting Others

With each Chicken Soup for the Soul book we publish, we designate a charity to receive a portion of the profits. A portion of the proceeds from *Chicken Soup for the Father and Son Soul* will be donated to the Synthesis Center.

The Synthesis Center is a nonprofit educational organization in Amherst, Massachusetts. The center offers a professional training program in psychosynthesis, a community counseling center, educational and support groups, workshops and business consulting.

Psychosynthesis is a spiritually oriented psychology whose assumptions support the view of the basic goodness of people, the promise of meaningful and purposeful lives, and the power of individuals, families, and communities to make changes in themselves and in their world. It is the hope and the day-to-day work of all of the people at the center to help create peace and health in every person and in the world. The center is committed to offering low-cost services to those in need.

For more information, to sign up for the center's e-newsletter, to be added to the mailing list, or to reach Dorothy Firman or Ted Slawski, please contact:

The Synthesis Center
274 North Pleasant St.
Amherst, MA 01002
413-256-0772
Website: www.synthesiscenter.org

Who Is Jack Canfield?

Jack Canfield is the cocreator and editor of the Chicken Soup for the Soul series, which *Time* magazine has called "the publishing phenomenon of the decade." The series now has 105 titles with over 100 million copies in print in forty-one languages. Jack is also the coauthor of eight other bestselling books, including *The Success Principles: How to Get from Where You Are to Where You Want to Be; Dare to Win; The Aladdin Factor; You've Got to Read This Book;* and *The Power of Focus: How to Hit Your Business and Personal and Financial Targets with Absolute Certainty.*

Jack has recently developed a telephone coaching program and an online coaching program based on his most recent book, *The Success Principles.* He also offers a seven-day Breakthrough to Success seminar every summer, which attracts 400 people from fifteen countries around the world.

Jack has conducted intensive personal and professional development seminars on the principles of success for over 900,000 people in twenty-one countries around the world. He has spoken to hundreds of thousands of others at numerous conferences and conventions and has been seen by millions of viewers on national television shows such as *The Today Show, Fox and Friends, Inside Edition, Hard Copy,* CNN's *Talk Back Live, 20/20, Eye to Eye,* the NBC *Nightly News,* and the CBS *Evening News.*

Jack is the recipient of many awards and honors, including three honorary doctorates and a Guinness World Records Certificate for having seven books from the Chicken Soup for the Soul series appearing on the *New York Times* bestseller list on May 24, 1998.

To write to Jack or for inquiries about Jack as a speaker, his coaching programs, or his seminars, use the following contact information:

The Canfield Companies
P.O. Box 30880 • Santa Barbara, CA 93130
Phone: 805-563-2935 • Fax: 805-563-2945
E-mail: info@jackcanfield.com
Website: www.jackcanfield.com

Who Is Mark Victor Hansen?

In the area of human potential, no one is more respected than Mark Victor Hansen. For more than thirty years, Mark has focused solely on helping people from all walks of life reshape their personal vision of what's possible. His powerful messages of possibility, opportunity, and action have created powerful change in thousands of organizations and millions of individuals worldwide.

He is a sought-after keynote speaker, bestselling author, and marketing maven. Mark's credentials include a lifetime of entrepreneurial success and an extensive academic background. He is a prolific writer with many bestselling books, such as *The One-Minute Millionaire, Cracking the Millionaire Code, How to Make the Rest of Your Life the Best of Your Life, The Power of Focus, The Aladdin Factor,* and *Dare to Win,* in addition to the Chicken Soup for the Soul series. Mark has had a profound influence through his library of audios, videos, and articles in the areas of big thinking, sales achievement, wealth building, publishing success, and personal and professional development.

Mark is the founder of the MEGA Seminar Series. MEGA Book Marketing University and Building Your MEGA Speaking Empire are annual conferences where Mark coaches and teaches new and aspiring authors, speakers, and experts on building lucrative publishing and speaking careers. Other MEGA events include MEGA Info-Marketing and My MEGA Life.

As a philanthropist and humanitarian, Mark works tirelessly for organizations such as Habitat for Humanity, American Red Cross, March of Dimes, Childhelp USA, and many others. He is the recipient of numerous awards that honor his entrepreneurial spirit, philanthropic heart, and business acumen. He is a lifetime member of the Horatio Alger Association of Distinguished Americans, an organization that honored Mark with the prestigious Horatio Alger Award for his extraordinary life achievements.

Mark Victor Hansen is an enthusiastic crusader of what's possible and is driven to make the world a better place.

Mark Victor Hansen & Associates, Inc.
P.O. Box 7665 • Newport Beach, CA 92658
Phone: 949-764-2640 • Fax: 949-722-6912
Website: www.markvictorhansen.com

Who Is Dorothy Firman?

Dr. Dorothy Firman is a professor, psychotherapist, life coach, author, consultant, speaker, and trainer. She has worked in the field of psychology for more than thirty years. Dorothy is a key-note speaker and offers workshops and seminars on a variety of topics. She has coauthored with her mother and sister *Chicken Soup for the Mother and Daughter Soul* and *Chicken Soup for the Soul, Celebrating Mothers and Daughters*. She has also coauthored *Daughters and Mothers, Healing the Relationship*. She has appeared on Oprah and many local and national television and radio programs.

Dorothy is a founding member of the Association for the Advancement of Psychosynthesis, a spiritual psychology that offers people the opportunity to deepen their experience of aliveness, presence, and the ability to serve. Through the Synthesis Center, a nonprofit educational organization cofounded by Jack Canfield in 1976, Dorothy has taught psychosynthesis to helping professionals for twenty-five years.

Dorothy has been married for over thirty years to her best friend and coauthor, Ted Slawski. They have worked together in a variety of settings and have three wonderful adult children and three incredible grandchildren.

For more on her work, visit The Synthesis Center Website. For more information on the mother-daughter work she does, visit the Mother-Daughter Website.

For more information contact, Dr. Firman at:

285 Pomeroy Lane
Amherst, MA 01002
413-256-3020
DFirman@comcast.net
www.synthesiscenter.org
www.motherdaughterrelations.com

Who Is Ted Slawski?

Ted is happily married to his coauthor Dorothy Firman. While this is Ted's first book, he has published several important works through the Synthesis Center Press, where he is a one-man show, from doing the layout, editing, and cover design through the final stages of publication. Ted is also a freelance computer consultant (Macs only!) and member of a small online business that sells Japanese samurai swords. Ted researches old swords and takes the photographs.

In his early life, Ted was a farmhand, factory worker, union steward, truck driver, and woodsman. Following that he spent twenty years as an automotive technician, then moved into computer diagnostics for cars, which led him to his work in computers.

Diagnosed with a chronic illness ten years ago, Ted, his wife, and his family have worked together to deal with health challenges, while he continues his roles as husband, father, son and working man. The love of family has stood him in good stead as he faces life's trials. His steadfast presence for all of his family has never wavered.

Ted and Didi (Dorothy) met when Ted was eighteen. The life they've lived together is the greatest gift each of them has. This book and the hard work that went into it is a loving tribute to this relationship.

For more information contact Ted at:
TSlawski@comcast.net

Contributors

Robert Anderson lives in Virginia Beach with his wife and son. He retired from the U.S. Navy in 2005 and still dreams of the ocean. Robert currently works for UHP Projects and enjoys his work. Robert can be reached at boba71@hotmail.com.

David Avrin is a marketing/branding consultant and an inspirational speaker. A part-time writer, he is the author of the popular book *The Gift in Every Day: Little Lessons on Living a Big Life* (2006 Sourcebooks). David's humorous and heartwarming presentations help audiences reflect, reconnect, and refuel. David can be reached at david@avrin.com.

Aaron Bacall has graduate degrees in organic chemistry and educational administration and supervision from New York University. He has been a pharmaceutical research chemist, college department coordinator, college instructor, and cartoonist. His work has appeared in most national publications, and he has been a contributor to several cartoon collections. His work has been used for advertising, greeting cards, wall calendars and several corporate promotional books. Three of his cartoons are featured in the permanent collection at the Harvard Business School's Baker Library. He continues to create and sell his cartoons. Aaron can be reached at abacall@msn.com.

Frederick Bakowski retired from the Federal Bureau of Prisons and is a member of the Emerald Coast Writers of Northwest Florida. He writes on a wide variety of subjects, including inspirational, nostalgic, and the paranormal. He enjoys falconry and Nathan's Coney Island hotdogs. Frederick can be reached at sleepymonk0716@aol.com.

Carl Ballenas is an award-winning teacher at Immaculate Conception School, Jamaica Estates, New York. As town historian, he coauthored books on Richmond Hill, New York, and Maple Grove Cemetery. He moderates his school's Aquinas Honor Society, which wrote the highly acclaimed Jacob Riis historical children's book, *Jacob's Gift*. Carl can be reached at cetus@mindspring.com.

Peter M. Balsino is a freelance writer and attorney living in Tucson, Arizona, with his wife and three children. He writes and speaks about lifestyle and simplification issues, and continues to strive to find the perfect balance between work and family life. He is available for writing and speaking. Peter can be reached at pmb@aronaz.com.

Melissa Moreau Baumann is a freelance author living in Chesapeake, Virginia. Matt is a Digital Media major at Marist College in Poughkeepsie, New York. This story is dedicated to the entire Moreau family, especially Katie Moreau— our amazing mother, grandmother, and friend. Melissa can be reached at melissabaumann@cox.net.

Martin Bucella is a full-time freelance cartoonist/humorous illustrator whose work has been published over 100,000 times through magazines, newspapers, greeting cards, books, the Internet, and more. To find out more about Marty's work, please visit http://members.aol.com/mjbtoons/index.html.

John P. Buentello is a teacher and writer. He is currently studying for a Ph.D. in English Literature. He is the coauthor of the novel *Reproduction Rights* and the short story collection *Binary Tales*. He writes for adults and children and is currently at work on a novel. John can be reached at jakkhakk@yahoo.com.

Martha Campbell is a graduate of Washington University of St. Louis School of Fine Arts and a former writer/designer for Hallmark Cards. She has been a freelance cartoonist and book illustrator since 1973. Martha can be reached at P.O. Box 2538, Harrison, AR 72602, or call 870-741-5323, or e-mail marthaf@alltel.net.

Tracy Crump lives in Mississippi with her husband, Stan. They homeschooled Brian (26) and Jeremy (22) for eleven years. Stan still enjoys his sons' company whenever possible, though paintball is the game of choice now. Tracy is a freelance writer and has published numerous articles. Tracy can be reached at tracygeneral@gmail.com.

Carl Dennison is a freelance writer from the Blue Ridge Mountains of western North Carolina. He received his Bachelor of Arts degree from the University of North Carolina at Chapel Hill in 1982. Carl enjoys reading, writing, gardening, photography, and spending time with his wife, Lou Ann.

Ted Diamond is a small-animal veterinarian and heretofore unpublished author. His wife Robin, who wrote for *Chicken Soup for the Mother and Son Soul* prompted him to tell this story. When he is not helping animals get healthy, Ted enjoys spending time with Robin and their three children, Jillian, Spencer and Jordan.

Bob Dickson is a professional writer from Southern California, where he lives with his wife and two daughters. He's written for the *LA Daily News,* Santa Clarita's *The Signal,* the *LA Times* newspaper group, and several magazines. He also teaches writing at The Master's College. Bob can be reached at Bob@BobsWordFactory.com.

Julie McMaine Evans, a Kentucky native and writer/PR consultant, sometimes writes about environmental issues. Her first husband, Wilton Accola, died in 1994 when an ice-laden limb fell on his car. She, son, David Accola, and husband, Jeffrey Evans, can be reached at julieeditor@gmail.com.

Dedicated to making a difference, **Susan Farr-Fahncke** is the creator of 2theheart.com and the founder of the amazing volunteer group Angels2TheHeart. She is the author of the beloved *Angel's Legacy* and has stories featured in numerous Chicken Soup books. To learn more about

Susan, or to sign up for one of her online writing workshops, please visit 2TheHeart.com.

Matthew Favreault grew up in Massachusetts, the youngest of five children. He landed in Eugene, Oregon, in 1995. He and his wife have three children. He hopes that Danielle, Jacob, and Misha will be inspired by the lessons that come from taking a walk with their dad.

Win Firman is a retiree after many active years in business, interrupted by three years as a bomb disposal officer in World War II. His volunteer work includes school board president, scoutmaster, and Little League president. Happily married for sixty-six years, Win has eight grandchildren and four great-grandchildren.

After a thirty-five year career in education, **Dorothy Fletcher** is presently enjoying her life of writing, motorcycle riding, and grandmothering. Her three books include *The Week of Dream Horses, The Cruelest Months,* and *Zen Fishing and Other Southern Pleasures.* To learn more about Dorothy, please visit www.dorothykfletcher.com.

John Forrest retired after thirty-four years as an educator and began writing about the exceptional events and wonderful people who have enriched his life. His story "The Gift of Time" was published in *Chicken Soup for the Christmas Soul* (2007). He lives in Orillia, Ontario, Canada, with his wife, Carol.

Sally Friedman, a frequent contributor to Chicken Soup for the Soul, is delighted to share her life with her husband, Victor, three daughters and sons-in-law, and seven grandchildren. She lives in Moorestown, New Jersey, and contributes to regional and national publications with her family as her inspiration. Sally can be reached at pinegander@aol.com.

Michael Fulton lives with his high school sweetheart, Marla, in the same neighborhood where they grew up. They have four children who are all active in sports. Michael has coached up to five teams a year in soccer, softball, and baseball since 1999. Daughters Ashley (age 19) and Amanda (age 17) are now coaching as well.

William Garvey (Bill) works as a damage prevention supervisor for a major Michigan utility. Bill lives for his family, loves writing, photography, auto restoration, and gardening. He is working on his first book about his inspirational journey of becoming a writer. To learn more about Bill, please visit HeartOfOurHeroes.com, or he can be reached at willyrain@mac.com.

Scott Gill is a pastor and freelance writer. He lives with his wife, Angela, and his four children in Rockwall, Texas. He is a graduate of the University of Memphis and Dallas Theological Seminary. He is currently studying writing for children through the Institute of Children's Literature.

Nancy Kay Grace is an inspirational writer and speaker for women's retreats and conferences. This is her second Chicken Soup for the Soul story. Nancy lives in northwest Arkansas, where her husband is a senior pastor. Please visit her website at www.nancygrace.com.

Bonnie Compton Hanson is author of several books for adults and children, including the popular Ponytail Girls series, plus hundreds of published articles and poems (twenty-four are included in Chicken Soup for the Soul books). She also speaks to MOPS, seniors, schools, and women's groups, and she leads writing seminars. Bonnie can be reached at bonnieh1@worldnet.att.net.

Patrick Hardin is a freelance cartoonist whose work appears in a variety of books and periodicals in the United States and abroad. He resides in his hometown of Flint, Michigan. He is a graduate of the University of Michigan–Flint, where he earned degrees in philosophy and psychology. Patrick can be reached at hardin_cartoons@comcast.net.

Charles E. Harrel pastored for thirty years before stepping down to pursue writing. He has over 160 published works. His stories and devotionals have appeared in eight books, including *The Embrace of a Father, Cup of Comfort Devotional,* and *Christian Miracles.* Charles enjoys teaching, playing guitar, and family camping trips.

Jonny Hawkins dedicates the cartoons in this book to his cousin Faith—who lives by her name—and her wonderful husband, Steve . . . and their rainbow of adopted children. Jonny's works, such as "Medical Cartoon-A-Day" and "Fishing Cartoon-A-Day" calendars, along with *A Joke a Day Keeps the Doctor Away,* are available everywhere. Jonny can be reached at jonnyhawkins2nz@yahoo.com.

Sherry Honeycutt Hatfield is a children's author and a graduate of the Institute of Children's Literature. She has also written for several Christian publications. Sherry and her loving husband are the parents of six precious children. She includes her maiden name in her pen name to honor her parents.

Louis A. Hill, Jr. authored three books and many articles. He earned a Ph.D. in structural engineering, designed bridges and buildings, and joined the engineering faculty at Arizona State University. He retired an Emeritus Dean of Engineering from the University of Akron. He is listed in *Who's Who in America.*

Miriam Hill is coauthor of *Fabulous Florida* and a frequent contributor to Chicken Soup for the Soul books. She's been published in the *Christian Science Monitor, Grit, St. Petersburg Times,* and Poynter Online. Miriam's manuscript received Honorable Mention for Inspirational Writing in the 75th Annual *Writer's Digest* Writing Competition.

Dennis Hixson grew up in the Northwest and has a bachelor's degree from the University of Idaho and a master's degree from Trinity Western University. He is currently the vice president of Pacific Life Bible College in Surrey, British Columbia. His wife and four children are his greatest treasure. Dennis enjoys his yearly humanitarian trips around the world, fly fishing, and gardening.

Pamela Hackett Hobson is a wife, mother of Tom and Mike, and author of two novels, *The Bronxville Book Club* and *The Silent,* and features in the *NY Times* article "Buzzz, Murmurs Follow Novel." To learn more about the author and her writing projects, please visit www.pamelahobson.com or send an e-mail to author@pamelaholbson.com.

Nancy Julien Kopp draws on everyday experiences for her creative nonfiction. Her work has been published in magazines, online, and in anthologies. She also writes children's fiction and articles about writing. She enjoys traveling, bridge, reading, and her four grandchildren. Nancy lives in Kansas with her retired husband.

Tom Krause is an international motivational speaker living in Missouri with wife, Amy, and sons, Tyler and Sam. To learn more about Tom, please visit www.krausespeaking.com.

Stephen Lautens has written a weekly column for the *Calgary Sun* since 1997. His columns have appeared in numerous other Canadian newspapers, and a collection was published as *A Chip off the Old Writer's Block.* He, his tolerant wife, and son live in Toronto. To learn more about Stephen and to read his columns, please visit www.lautens.com.

John J. Lesjack, a graduate of East Detroit High School and San Francisco State University, is a retired grade school teacher and active freelance writer. His works have appeared in many national publications—*Instructor, Science of Mind, Reminisce,* and *Chicken Soup for the Chocolate Lover's Soul.* John can be reached at Jlesjack@gmail.com.

Patricia Lorenz, an art-of-living writer and much sought-after speaker, is the author of nine books, including *Life's Too Short to Fold Your Underwear.* She's one of the top contributing writers to the Chicken Soup for the Soul books with stories in over thirty editions. Patricia lives in Largo, Florida, where she loves the freedom to follow her dreams while she's still awake. To contact her about speaking to your group, Patricia can be reached at patricialorenz@juno.com.

Patrick Lyons received his Bachelor of Science from Florida A&M University, and Master of Science in Management from North Carolina State University. He is author of *Map Your Financial Future: Starting the Right Path in Your Teens and Twenties.* To learn more about Patrick, please visit www.mapyourfinancialfuture.com.

Tim Martin is the author of four books and seven screenplays. His script *Fast Pitch* is presently in preproduction at Promenade Pictures, and his novel, *The*

Culverts of Humbolt County, is due out this fall. Tim can be reached at tmartin@northcoast.com.

Tom Miller is a former history professor and novelist. His latest novel is *Full Court Press* (2000). He is a columnist for Military.com. Tom can be reached at tmillercshaw@msn.com.

Gary W. Moore is the author of *Playing with the Enemy*, CEO of AQUAtiva, a motivational speaker, and musician. Gary is married to Arlene, his wife of 32 years. Contact Gary at: gmoore@playingwiththeenemy.com.

Mark Musolf is a graduate of Western Illinois University. Mark grew up in the Midwest and has lived in Illinois, Indiana, Wisconsin, and currently resides in Minnesota. He enjoys working on his home, being with his wife and two sons, and traveling whenever possible. Mark can be reached at jhmusolf@aol.com.

Mark Parisi's "off the mark" comic, syndicated since 1987, is distributed by United Media. Mark's humor also graces greeting cards, T-shirts, calendars, magazines, newsletters, and books. Lynn is his wife and business partner. Their daughter, Jen, contributes with inspiration, (as do three cats). To learn more about Mark, please visit offthemark.com.

Helen Kay Polaski is an author and editor. Her most recent projects include editing the anthology books *Christmas Memories, Stories to Warm the Heart and Renew the Spirit, A Cup of Comfort for Weddings,* and *Classic Christmas, True Stories of Holiday Cheer and Goodwill.* Helen can be reached at hkpolaski@yahoo.com.

Michael T. Powers, whose writing appears in twenty-seven inspirational books, including many in the Chicken Soup series, is a youth pastor, motivational speaker, high school girls coach, founder of HeartTouchers.com, and author of his own book, *Heart Touchers*. To learn more about Michael, to read more of his writing, or to join the thousands of world-wide readers on his inspirational website, please visit http://www.HeartTouchers.com, or he can be reached at HeartTouchers@aol.com.

Dave Quist received his bachelor's degree in psychology from Northern Arizona University in Flagstaff, Arizona. Dave enjoys cycling, swimming, and weight lifting. He lives in Tucson, Arizona, with his wife and son.

Andy Radujko would like to dedicate this story to two truly amazing, incredible people he calls Mom and Dad. Without Steve and Janis Marcy, Andy's life would have been incredibly different. Thanks, I love you both very much.

Robert C. Raina studied art at the University of Massachusetts at Amherst. He is a cartoonist and has written and illustrated several books for children. Robert is the president and owner of a full time entertainment company located in Western Massachusetts (bobrainadj.com). He can be contacted at robertraina@cox.net and his writing and art work can be viewed at bobrainawriting.com.

Randy Richardson's debut mystery novel, *Lost in the Ivy*, and humorous musings on parenting have received numerous awards as well as praise from his family. An attorney and president of the Chicago Writers Association, he lives in Illinois with his wife, son, and cat. To learn more about Randy, please visit www.lostintheivy.com.

Calvin Riendeau was a single father of two sons for about ten years. It had many challenges and many more rewards than he had imagined. Calvin's first priority was to teach them to be good people, to treat others with compassion and dignity, and that respect is an earned privilege. He can only hope that they have learned as much from him as he has from them. As they are now young adults they have a great bond of friendship that Calvin defines as family.

Glenn Rifkin is a journalist and author living near Boston. He has written extensively for the *New York Times* and has authored ten books, including *Thoreau's Backyard: Musings from a Small Town*. Glenn has a son, Benjamin, and two stepchildren, Cameron and Laura. Glenn can be reached at grifkin@comcast.net.

Bruce Robinson is an award-winning internationally published cartoonist whose work has appeared in numerous consumer and trade periodicals including the *National Enquirer, The Saturday Evening Post, Woman's World, The Sun, First, Highlights for Children*, etc. He is also author of the cartoon book *GOOD MEDICINE*. Contact him at: cartoonsbybrucerobinson@hotmail.com.

Sallie A. Rodman received her certificate in Professional Writing at California State University Long Beach. She has won awards from *Writer's Digest* and *Byline* for her inspirational stories. Her work appears in numerous Chicken Soup editions and various magazines and newspapers. She also has a story on Chicken Soup dog food bags. Sallie can be reached at sa.rodman@verizon.net.

Carol S. Rothchild received her master's degree in writing from Johns Hopkins University. She is the senior features editor of *SIX78th*, the junior high lifestyle magazine. She is most passionate about writing for children and young adults. When she is not writing, she is usually behind a camera.

Tracey Sherman is a three-time contributor to the Chicken Soup series. She is wife to her best friend/soulmate of twenty-seven years, mother to three wonderful children, grandmother to one. She continues to strive toward her dream of publishing for children and young adults. Tracey can be reached at ShermanTL@aol.com.

Besides raising three boys, **Sarah Smiley** is the author of *Going Overboard* (Penguin/NAL, 2005) and is a syndicated newspaper columnist. To learn more about Sarah, please visit www.SarahSmiley.com.

Bob Smith graduated from the University of Baltimore in 1996 with a Bachelor of Science. He is a recreation and parks professional in Baltimore County,

Maryland. Bob lives in the town of Edgemere with his wife, Shannon, and their two children, Hannah and Connor.

Christine Mae Smith is a mother of three, grandmother of thirteen, and foster mother of numerous others. She is a frequent contributor to Chicken Soup for the Soul books and has had stories published in *Woman's World* magazine and in two monthly newsletters. Christine enjoys reading, writing, and spending time with family.

John Spatola grew up in Brooklyn and loved to play baseball with his dad. He is currently an accountant and life insurance salesman. He is married and has two sons. He now plays golf and, by the way, coached his sons' baseball teams. He was so moved by the Chicken Soup for the Soul books, he had to share his story.

Gloria Cassity Stargel writes for *Guideposts*, Chicken Soul for the Soul, and others. Her award-winning book, *The Healing: One Family's Victorious Struggle with Cancer*, strengthens faith, gives hope. To learn more about Gloria or to read portions of her book, please visit www.brightmorning.com. You can also order online, or call 1-800-888-9529, or order through the mail: Applied Images, 312 Bradford St. NW, Gainesville, GA 30501.

Ken Swarner is author of *Whose Kids Are These Anyway?* Ken can be reached at kenswarner@aol.com.

Andrew Toos has established a national reputation through his offbeat lifestyle cartoons for clients, such as *Reader's Digest, Saturday Evening Post, Gallery Stern, Accountancy, Baseball Digest, CEO* magazine, the *Washington Post, Barron's,* Bayer Corp., *Good Housekeeping, Cosmopolitan,* and many other titles and media outlets. His work is licensed through CartoonResource.com. Andrew lives with his wife, Nancy, in Florida.

Ed VanDeMark has a Bachelor of Science in Art Education. He's worked in county government in upstate New York for more than thirty-three years. He is married, the father of three adult children, and grandfather of four grandsons and two granddaughters. Ed enjoys church activities, writing, cartooning, lawn work, and sports.

Donald Verkow lives with his wife of thirty-two years, Katie, and his labs, Molly and Abby. He is assistant principal at Paramount Charter Academy in Kalamazoo. Don loves to travel, enjoys the beach, writes and plays golf. Don is the author of several short stories.

Since 1990, **Joseph Walker** has written a weekly newspaper column called "ValueSpeak." Some of his columns were published in *Chicken Soup for the Grandparent's Soul, Chicken Soup for the Teacher's Soul,* and *Chicken Soup for the Mother and Son Soul.* His books include *Look What Love Has Done* for Deseret Book. Joseph and his wife, Anita, have five children and four grandchildren.

Nick Walker is a meteorologist and host of *First Outlook* weekday mornings on The Weather Channel. He presents educational programs to young people and hosts the Weather Dude website at www.wxdude.com. A singer-songwriter, Nick's recording "Sing Along with the Weather Dude" teaches basic weather concepts through music.

Stephen Wayne resides in northern New Jersey, is a husband, father, and a first-time contributor to a Chicken Soup anthology. A former police detective who specialized and lectured on juvenile and family matters, he now shares his thoughts through his writings and has appeared in various publications. Contact: stephenrusinaiak@yahoo.com.

Bob Weber was born and reared in Arden Hills, a northern suburb of St. Paul, Minnesota. As a youth, he actively participated in Boy Scouts, 4-H, and Junior Achievement. Majoring in Speech and Communications at the University of Minnesota, Bob went on to a thirty-five year career in sales and marketing. Now retired, he designs and builds award-winning furniture, writes funding proposals for area charites, and currently is director of Sport Support 4 Kids, a program that provides funds for low-income kids, which allows them to participate in local athletic programs.

By day, **David Wilkins** is a vice president of Manufacturing Operations at Aragon Surgical. At night, he's an author of previous Chicken Soup for the Soul stories and is currently seeking an agent for his completed novel. He earned his Bachelor of Arts in Management from St. Mary's College in Moraga, California. Since 1976 he has lived in San Jose with his British wife. David can be reached at bestseller2005@yahoo.com.

June Williams lives in Brush Prairie, Washington, with her husband, Mac. She enjoys her family and writing stories about them. Her work has appeared in six Chicken Soup books. June can be reached at june.williams@comcast.net.

Paul Winick, M.D., lives in Hollywood, Florida, with his wife of forty-four years, Dorothy. He practiced pediatrics there for almost thirty years. He has two married children; Charles, who is married to Maureen (children—triplets—Jordan, Toby, and Samantha), and Ruth, who is married to Frank (children, Martina and Bryan). Dr. Winick graduated from Columbia College and SUNY Downstate Medical Center School of Medicine. Presently, he is a full professor of clinical pediatrics at the University of Miami School of Medicine.

Ferida Wolff is a contributor to several Chicken Soup books. She writes books for children and adults, including the picture book *Is a Worry Worrying You?* and the essay book *The Adventures of Swamp Woman: Menopause Essays on the Edge.* To learn more about Ferida, please visit www.feridawolff.com.

Woody Woodburn has been a frequent contributor to the Chicken Soup for the Soul series. A sports journalist for more than twenty-five years, he is currently working on his first nonsports book. He lives in Ventura, California. Woody can be reached at Woodywoodburn99@aol.com.

Gary Xavier is a lecturer and author of engineering textbooks and a newspaper columnist. He and his wife, Linda, have two grown sons. His column is based on his students, his life with his family, and the nine dogs that have been part of their lives. Gary can be reached at gary_xavier@yahoo.com.

Thousands of **Bob Zahn**'s cartoons have been published in all the leading publications. He has more than one thousand greeting cards to his credit, as well as several humor books. Bob can be reached at zahntoons@aol.com, or to learn more about him, please visit, www.zahntoons.com.

Lanny Zechar is a writer and speaker living in Southern California with his family. His story "Trust Me" was published in the *Chicken Soup for the Father & Daughter Soul*. Lanny's future plans include publishing a novel and several children's stories.